ROYAL BOROUGH OF KENSINGTON & CHELSEA

This book must be returned to the Library named above on or
before the latest date below. Adult readers will be charged fines
on books kept beyond that date. The period of loan will be
extended if the book is brought to the Library for re-dating
providing that it is not required by another reader.

15. JUN 88	30. MAY 89	29. MAY
18. JUN 88	29. JUL 89	
18. JUL 88		08. JUN 90
15. AUG 88		
27. SEP 88	08. SEP 82	
01. NOV 88		
06. DEC 88		
19. JAN 89	28. OCT 89	
03. FEB 89	07. NOV 89	
31. MAR 89	02 JAN 90	
03. MAY 89	01. FEB 90	
	22. MAR 90	

Books which have been exposed to infection from any
infectious disease must NOT be returned to the Library but
sent at once to the Environmental Health Officer or handed to
one of his Inspectors.

E1/41

HEALING OILS AND ESSENCES

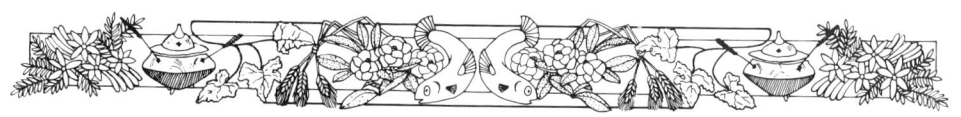

By the same authors:
An Illustrated Dictionary of Natural Health

By Nevill Drury:
The Healing Power
Inner Health (ed.)
The Bodywork Book (ed.)
Healers, Quacks or Mystics?
Music for Inner Space
Vision Quest

HEALING OILS
AND ESSENCES

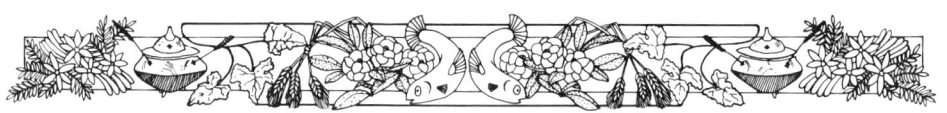

Nevill and Susan Drury

ROBERT HALE · LONDON

Note to readers

None of the health remedies mentioned in this book should be regarded as a substitute for orthodox medical treatment. This book presents the views of alternative natural therapists and does not guarantee the medicinal effectiveness of their remedies. Nevertheless, it is our view that the field of essential oils and flower essences warrants serious scientific and medical investigation.

© Nevill and Susan Drury Publishing Pty Limited 1987

First published in Great Britain 1988

ISBN 0 7090 3268 4

Robert Hale Limited
Clerkenwell House
Clerkenwell Green
London EC1R 0HT

Typeset by Graphicraft Typesetters Ltd, Hong Kong
Printed by Kyodo Printing Company, Singapore

CONTENTS

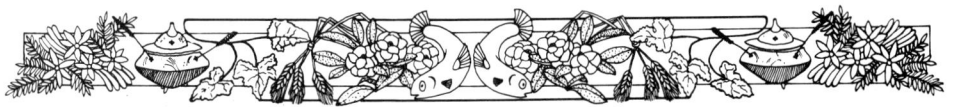

ACKNOWLEDGEMENTS

Thanks are due to several individuals and organisations for information included in this book. These include: Blackmores Communications (herbal oils and essential fatty acids); Muir & Neil Ltd (essential fatty acids and evening primrose oil); Thursday Plantation (tea-tree oil); Triad (essential oils and incenses); Dr Edward Bach Healing Society, Flower Essence Society, Santa Fe Flower Connection, Inc., Ian and Kristin White, Roy Victor Love, and Living Essences (flower essences), and also the resource archives of *Nature & Health* magazine.

PREFACE

It is always rewarding to focus on the essence of something, and in the case of this book we have had the intriguing task of bringing together information relating to the essential oils in plants and the essential fatty acids occurring in various edible oils.

Perhaps the main point we would like to get across here, the views of the late Nathan Pritikin notwithstanding, is that there are good oils and bad oils, good fats and bad fats, and it is important for all of us to be able to recognise and utilise them.

Certainly, it would seem that such a book is timely. There is increasing international interest in the natural health therapies — particularly because they emphasise self-help and preventive healthcare — and several natural modalities utilise essential oils. Herbal oils feature, for example, in massage and aromatherapy (which in turn encompasses natural hair and skin care) and a study of healthy food oils is essential in any study of diet and nutrition. Indeed, the healing oils play a vital role in all healing arts which draw on the rich resources of Nature.

Plants and foods were man's earliest form of natural medicine and retain their value today. More and more people are turning to non-drug, non-chemical sources of health treatment and only recently have we realised how important the polyunsaturated fatty acids are in combating heart disease. It is also true that in western society we have become increasingly aware of the role of stress and negative emotions in creating disease. The Bach flower remedies and other wildflower essences treat illness as a form of vibrational imbalance and introduce us to the mental and spiritual dimensions of health which are often as important as the outer physical symptoms.

We had all these factors in mind when researching this book, and hope it will prove useful as an introduction to healing oils and essences. Good health!

Nevill and Susan Drury

HERBAL OILS

INTRODUCTION

For centuries aromatic plants have been used in healing and in religious ceremonies. In ancient Egypt myrrh was offered to Ra, rose petals were placed in the tombs of pharoahs to perfume their journey to the afterworld, and coriander was employed in funeral rites. The Hebrews used hyssop as a deodorant to purify their temples and both galbanum and frankincense as a special offering in their sacred ceremonies, while the Greeks favoured anise to ward off bad dreams and to ease coughs and colds. Hippocrates was especially fond of garlic as a remedy for indigestion and Arabian physicians prescribed chamomile as a general panacea. So, healing plants have been with us since the birth of civilisation and have been prized for their essential oils and unique fragrances.

Today this tradition continues in the art of aromatherapy — the therapeutic use of essential oils. Practitioners believe that each of these oil has vital properties because it represents the 'soul of the plant', its 'lifeforce', or its 'heart essence'. There is undoubtedly a certain mystique in all this, for many of the flower oils used in aromatherapy are exotic — like ylang-ylang — or have romantic associations — like lavender, rose and sandalwood.

However, aromatherapy is becoming increasingly recognised as a form of complementary medicine, and in modern times a few notable pioneers have considerably advanced our knowledge of essential oils.

The term 'aromatherapy' was in fact coined by the French scientist, Professor René Maurice Gattefossé, who discovered the beneficial effects of plant essences by accident. Gattefossé was working in his laboratory and burned his hand while engaged in an experiment. A dish of lavender oil was nearby and he used it to soothe his hand, and was amazed at the speed with which his burn healed. Gattefossé later noted that such essences could be used as cosmetic agents and also to treat skin conditions like dermatitis. They also seemed to possess anti-bacterial qualities and could therefore be potentially useful against infections.

A colleague of Gattefossé, M. Goddissart, established an aromatherapy clinic in Los Angeles and developed a treatment for skin cancers using lavender oil. In 1938 he also reported that he was obtaining excellent results in using essences to treat gangrene, osteomalacia, wounds and facial ulcers — all of which were healing in rapid time.

Dr Jean Valnet, who authored the influential book *The Practice of Aromatherapy*, also used similar techniques to Goddissart during the second world war to heal wounds and scars. More recently the French biochemist Madame Marguerite Maury developed the techniques of applying plant essences for 'rejuvenation'. She found that aromatherapy stimulated the reproduction of skin cells and restored the elasticity of muscle tissue, enabling the skin to remain healthy and comparatively unwrinkled. Mme Maury also believed that the abundant free electrons of aromatic essences were able to influence physiological functions and that it was by this method rather than some chemical process that the oils actually worked. In 1962 she was awarded the Prix International d'Esthetique and in 1967 the CIDESCO Prize for her work on aromatherapy preparations.

Since that time the pioneering work of the French aromatherapists has been continued by such modern practitioners as Danièle Ryman, who opened the Marguerite Maury Clinic in London, British therapist Shirley Price, who has a practice in Burbage, Leicestershire, and the distinguished writer Robert Tisserand has used essential oils in his practice for over a decade.

The properties of essential oils

Essential oils are volatile and evaporate readily, dispersing their scent into the air. They are also antibiotic, antiseptic, anti-viral and anti-inflammatory in varying degrees. Most are colourless but some are quite distinctive in appearance: for example, cinnamon is red, chamomile blue and wormwood green. Most are lighter than water — garlic is an exception — and the essential oils dissolve in a variety of liquids, including cider vinegar, honey, ethyl alcohol, and vegetable oils like sunflower seed, sweet almond, avocado and grapeseed. They are also absorbed into vegetable fats and beeswax.

Understandably, essential oils are very expensive, because it may take 200 kilograms of fresh flowers to produce 1 kilogram of essential oil. Nevertheless, essential oils have a wide range of uses in cosmetic skin and beauty care, massage, and in treatments for such complaints as respiratory infections, indigestion, influenza, constipation, headaches, cuts and bruises, and various muscular disorders.

When used in massage, for example, the essential oil penetrates the skin and the aroma is also pleasant and relaxing, helping to relieve stress and tension. However, many of the essential oils also have specific medicinal properties which lend themselves to therapeutic use:

Some are antiseptics The terpenes, phenols, alcohols and aldehydes provide these properties, and examples include lemon, thyme, tea-tree and garlic.

Some are anti-viral These may work against such complaints as influenza. Examples include cinnamon, pine, thyme and lemon.

Some are helpful for wounds and abrasions These include lavender, sage, thyme, rosemary and tea-tree.

Some are stimulants These include pine, basil and rosemary (for the adrenals), mint and anise (for the anterior pituitary body) and cinnamon, ylang-ylang, jasmine and sandalwood (for sexual responsiveness).

Some affect milk-supply in lactating women Anise, caraway and fennel *promote* lactation; parsley, mint and sage *reduce* milk supply.

Some have anti-inflammatory properties These include cajeput, chamomile, lavender, rose, sandalwood and tea-tree.

Some are distinctly calming Among these are bergamot, chamomile, cypress, geranium, hyssop, juniper, rose, lavender and ylang-ylang.

Essential oils are extracted from plants in different ways:

Pressing by hand

This method is generally used for plants in the citrus family, like oranges, lemons, bergamots and limes. The rinds are squeezed by hand until the oil glands burst, yielding the essential oil. (Incidentally, orange is an interesting example of a plant that yields different essences. Oil of orange is extracted from the rind, neroli derives from the flowers, and petitgrain from the leaves.)

Enfleurage

Here the flowers are spread in a glass dish which contains purified fat. The flowers are left for up to 72 hours, allowing their perfume to soak into the fat, and are then replaced with fresh blooms. The process continues until the fat is saturated with essential oil — it is then referred to as a pomade. This pomade may be dissolved in alcohol — actually the fat itself does not dissolve but the essential oil does. The resulting liquid can then be heated gently. The alcohol evaporates first, leaving the essential oil intact in the container.

Maceration

This method resembles enfleurage and utilises vegetable oil or fat to

5

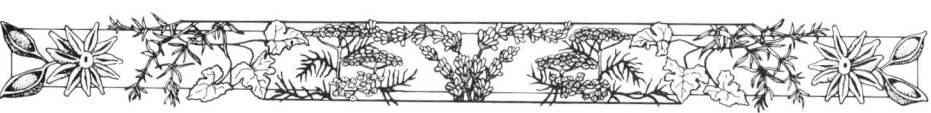

absorb the essential oil from the flowers. The process of renewing the flowers may take several months, and vegetable oils impregnated with essential oil in this way are ideal for massage.

Distillation

There are different methods of distillation. With the open-fire process there is always a risk of burning the plants, so the favoured methods involve steam or vacuum distillation. Steam is passed over the leaves or flowers and the essential oil vaporises. The steam is later cooled and the essential oil condenses. Because the latter is not water-soluble it can be easily collected.

Dissolving

In some instances solvents like alcohol or petrol ether can be used. Alcohol is utilised to extract gums and resins like galbanum and myrrh while petrol ether is used with fresh flowers and plants. In the latter case, the flowers are covered with the solvent to extract the essential oil and the solvent is then evaporated — leaving the essential oil behind.

Essential oils are sensitive to light and temperature. Ideally they should be stored in dark, air-tight glass bottles and kept in a cool location (approximately 18°C or 65°F). Pure essential oils will keep for around 18–24 months but do not last as long when mixed in a vegetable oil. In this instance, the oil begins to oxidise and turn rancid, so new batches of massage oil, for example, should be prepared every couple of months or so. The best carrier oils have no odour of their own. English aromatherapist Shirley Price recommends avocado, grapeseed, hazelnut and wheatgerm as ideal for masage, in combination with the selected essential oil (Price, 1983:97).

Uses of essential oils

Apart from massage there are four other main ways in which essential oils may be used:

Inhalation

Use a special nose-dropper, or alternatively put ten drops of essential oil on a handkerchief and inhale repeatedly from it. The handkerchief can also be placed beside the pillow at night, to facilitate easier breathing. It may also be good to make a 'steam bath' by placing ten drops of essential oil into 100 ml of hot water. Drape a towel over your head and also over the basin, and breathe deeply, face over the water, until the aroma has disappeared. Do this three times a day.

Ideal for: headaches, blocked sinuses, coughs and sore throats.

Taken internally

One of the best ways is to take the essential oil in 'honey water'. Dissolve a teaspoon of honey in a glass of warm water and then add one to three drops of essential oil. Take two to three times daily. Alternatively, add two drops of essential oil to a pot of weak tea prepared with one teabag only.
Ideal for: coughs and colds, headaches, indigestion and constipation.

In baths

Place ten to fifteen drops of essential oil in your bath and make sure you remain in the water for at least a quarter of an hour. Some essential oils are relaxing — chamomile, lavender, rose or marjoram. Other oils like basil, peppermint, juniper, hyssop or rosemary have a stimulating effect.
Ideal for: insomnia, tension, muscular disorders, circulatory complaints, headaches, coughs and colds.

In compresses

Make a compress using a solution of ten drops of essential oil in 100 ml of water. The compress should then be left in position over the affected area for two to four hours.
Ideal for: bruises, wounds and sprains, chest pains and skin problems.

Many different essential oils are now available, and the plants and flowers from which they are extracted have many distinctive properties. The following listings include most of the more familiar herbal oils and provide a cogent reminder that Nature has provided us with many wonderful healing remedies. Indeed, as Marguerite Maury once said, the aromatic extracts of plants are the 'purest form of living energy' available to us in the healing process.

ALOE VERA

Aloe barbadenisis

According to a Hindu legend the aloe vera plant came directly from the Garden of Paradise. The ancient Egyptians called it 'the plant of immortality' and Cleopatra and Nefertiti are reputed to have used its gel to maintain their beauty. It is mentioned in the Psalms of Solomon, Roman writings describe its medicinal applications, and soldiers in Alexander the Great's armies used it to treat their wounds. Aloe vera, indeed, has a variety of uses, for it can be used to treat gastritis, peptic ulcers, respiratory infections, arthritis, burns, mouth ulcers, insect bites, cuts, blisters, abrasions, muscle cramps and pain in the joints.

Aloe vera resembles a cactus, but is actually a perennial succulent which belongs to the lily family. It is one of a class of plants called xerophytes, which are able to close their pores in order to avoid loss of water. The leaves are stiff and fleshy with spiny edges. A mature leaf may weigh up to 500 grams, and it is the pulp or gel within the leaf which is used in cosmetics and medicinal preparations — for the gel contains 'biogenic stimulators'. Ninety-six per cent of the gel is water, but the remaining four per cent includes polysaccharides like glucose and mannose. These carbohydrates, in conjunction with the water content, moisturise the skin. Other constituents of aloe vera pulp include the natural healer chrysophanic acid, antiseptic saponins and enzymes which combat inflammation. Interestingly, when a leaf is broken from the plant, the wound quickly seals and the plant retains its vital, healing properties.

However, aloe vera also contains a bitter sap, or juice, called aloin, and there is a difference between aloin and aloe gel. Aloe gel derives from the thin-walled cells of the leaves, but the juice comes from the cells immediately below the skin and it is this bitter extract which is used in the cosmetic industry as a sunscreen. Aloin contains barbaloin, an anthraquinone glycoside, and should not be taken internally since it may cause a purging effect which can be harmful. For this reason, aloe vera should not be self-medicated without naturopathic or medical advice.

Practical applications

Soaps, cleansers and moisturisers containing aloe vera may be used to decrease the severity of acne in conjunction with a balanced diet and good personal hygiene. Similarly, aloe vera is useful for treating tinea — it can be rubbed into the affected area at least four times a day and it is ideal for aches, cuts, cramps and burns. It reduces the chance of infection and will also reduce the likelihood of sunburn.

Shampoos containing at least 70 per cent aloe vera gel are beneficial for the health of the hair and scalp.

The gel is useful for treating digestive disorders, and when taken internally can be used for ulcers, colitis, constipation and inflammatory bowel complaints. However, all internal applications of aloe vera require medical advice.

ANISE (ANISEED)

Pimpinella anisum

Anise seeds have been a highly prized commodity for several centuries and were known and valued in ancient Egypt, Greece and Rome. In Biblical times, when the Romans levied heavy taxes in return for the protection they gave to the subjects of their vast empire, these taxes were often paid in precious herbs and spices. Two of these most commonly mentioned were anise and mint. The ancient Greeks had a high regard for the medicinal qualities of anise, especially for coughs and colds and even for bad dreams. Indeed, the mathematician Pythagoras actually claimed it was possible to ward off a seizure by holding on to an anise plant.

In Roman times anise was widely used as a digestive aid, something which was especially necessary after their enormous banquets. Anise and other spices were baked into a special cake which was served at the end of a feast to ease the discomfort of those who had eaten. This cake is thought by some to be an antecedent of our modern spicy wedding cakes.

Anise is a feathery-leafed annual herb native to the Middle East. It grows best in a sheltered sunny spot and the slender stems should reach a height of 40-50 cm. The early leaves of the plant are quite rounded but these are followed by more feathery carrot-like leaves and flat, white flower heads which bloom in late summer. These produce small, brown, aromatic seeds or fruit, each of which has a fine hair at one end. The plant is ready to harvest when the seed heads are heavy and the stems beginning to yellow. They can be cut and dried in the sun and the seeds removed from the husks simply by rubbing and sifting through a sieve. These licorice-tasting seeds are often used in cooking, especially to flavour cakes and pastries, rich cheese or pork dishes and also vegetables which can be rather indigestible. The essential oil extracted from them contains estragole (methylchavicol), choline, terpenes and resins as well as the most important substance, anethole, which has a beneficial effect on digestion. It should be used with care, in small doses only, for it has narcotic qualities which slow the circulation and may cause circulatory and cerebral disorders. It is an excellent carminative, helpful for all sorts of indigestion, flatulence and infant colic, and is used to flavour liqueurs such as Anisette, perhaps partly because of its function as a digestive aid.

Oil of anise is a pleasant-smelling and effective antiseptic, and is used to make mouth washes and breath sweeteners. It is often used to flavour cough lozenges and is additionally helpful because of its antispasmodic properties. Anise oil has also been recommended for nervous vomiting, nauseous migraine, palpitations of the heart and any breathing difficulty which is due to bronchial spasms. It can be used to increase the milk flow of nursing mothers. Especially when mixed with oil of sassafras, anise oil can be used as an insect repellent.

There is a variant of anise which originated in China known as Chinese Star (*Illicium verum*). Its oil is rich in anethole and has a similar chemical composition to common anise. Indeed it is Chinese Star which is most commonly used in commercial pharmaceutical preparations which call for anise, although it is not usually recommended for home aromatherapy because of its potentially harmful side-effects.

Practical application

Many types of indigestion can be alleviated by taking a small glass of aniseed liqueur after the evening meal. This can be made from one litre of spirits to which have been added 40 g crushed aniseeds, 1 g cinnamon and 500 g sugar. The mixture should be left to macerate for six weeks then filtered and bottled.

Alternatively Chinese Star can be used in a restricted dose of one drop on sugar taken twice a day after meals.

Nursing mothers can take two drops of anise oil on a little sugar three times a day to increase their milk supply. For coughs and bronchial spasms three drops of oil can be taken on sugar three times a day.

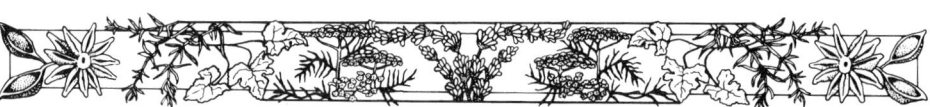

BASIL (SWEET BASIL)

Ocimum basilicum

There are over 150 different species of basil, some of which are highly aromatic — hence the generic name *ocimum* which is based on a Greek word meaning 'to smell'. Sweet basil was originally grown in India where it was known as *tulsi* and regarded as sacred to Krishna and Vishnu. It has been widely used there since the Vedic period and is highly valued for its medicinal qualities.

Basil was also known in ancient Egypt, Greece and Rome and was introduced to England in the sixteenth century where it was used as a strewing herb and powdered to make snuff. The ancient Greeks associated the plant with hatred and believed it would only grow if the seeds were sown with a certain amount of abuse. The plant has often been associated with poison and venomous beasts, though in India it was used as a remedy for snake bites and scorpion stings. One of the many legends surrounding the fragrant basil plant concerns its alleged ability to judge chastity. If a sprig is worn by anyone who is not a virgin it is said to shrivel and die immediately. In Italy and other Mediterranean countries basil is a symbol of love, and in parts of Lebanon a pot of basil placed on the window sill is associated with courtship.

Sweet basil, the best-known variety and the one most commonly used in the kitchen (especially in combination with tomatoes), has soft, very bright green leaves and may grow up to 75 cm tall. It is highly sensitive to frost and will shrivel and die in cold weather. In hot climates it may flourish all year.

The best time to harvest the plant is just before the small white-edged flowers are in full bloom. The long, leafy stalks are cut, and the essence extracted by steam distillation. This produces a pale greenish-yellow oil with a light pleasant odour — a bit like a cross between peppermint and thyme — and has a slightly bitter taste. This oil is rich in estragol, linalol, lineol, ocimene and camphor.

It makes a very good aromatic nerve tonic which clears the head, strengthens and sharply focuses the mind and reduces mental fatigue. It can be used for a variety of nervous disorders including anxiety, insomnia, migraine, hysteria, depression and a general inability to make decisions and take action.

Basil is also an antispasmodic, useful in relieving indigestion and dyspepsia which are caused by gastric spasms and for asthma, whooping cough, epilepsy, muscular spasms and hiccups.

It is an antiseptic and expectorant which, though not as valuable as eucalyptus, can be used in the treatment of respiratory diseases such as bronchitis, emphysema, chronic colds and catarrh. It is sometimes used to reduce fevers, particularly those which are partly induced by the mind or emotions.

Used externally it is an effective insect repellent, especially for mosquitoes and can be applied to ease the pain of stings, particularly wasp stings. In India it has been used in small quantities as a skin tonic and freshener for sluggish and congested complexions with enlarged pores.

Practical application

For anxiety, depression and other nervous conditions, three to five drops of oil of basil should be taken on a little sugar or in an alcoholic solution three times a day. Nervous indigestion and gastric spasms can be relieved by taking a half to one teaspoon of antispasmodic syrup after each meal. This syrup can be made by mixing 1g essence of basil with 1g essence of marjoram and 50g sugar. It can be even more effective when stirred into a cup of herbal tea made from either verbena or lime blossom. Externally, basil oil can be applied directly to insect stings or, if preferred, mixed with 3 per cent sweet almond oil.

BENZOIN

Styrax benzoin

Also known as friar's balsam and gum benjamin, benzoin is a balsamic resin which is exuded from trees of the genus Styrax. It is one of the classic ingredients of incense, and in ancient times was burnt to drive away evil spirits. Some people still use it today as the scent-essence in seances to summon the spirits of the dead by incantation. For several centuries the Chinese have imported benzoin to use for medicinal purposes, and it has been known in Europe at least since the sixteenth century though it was not used by many of the early herbalists, perhaps because they found it difficult to obtain.

The trees are grown in Java, Sumatra and Thailand. Gum benzoin is not produced naturally but forms when a deep cut is made in the trunk of a tree causing a slow exudation which hardens into a greyish-coloured gum with dark red streaks. These streaks contain the highest concentration of aromatic material. It is further processed to yield a resin with a pleasant odour, rather like vanilla, which is a rich reddish-colour with the consistency of a fatty oil. Like all true resins it contains benzoic acid, an important preservative and antiseptic which is used extensively in the manufacturing of medicines, plastics, dyes, cosmetics and insect repellents. A little more than 500 grams of resin can be obtained from each tree which is higher than 20 metres.

Benzoin is a stimulant and antiseptic. A drop placed on the tongue will produce a hot burning sensation followed by a pleasant feeling of warmth which flows throughout the body. It is best known for its use as an expectorant invaluable for all kinds of respiratory disorders such as colds, flu, asthma and bronchitis. Taken internally through inhalation it encourages the expulsion of mucus and so clears the lungs, making breathing easier.

Benzoin also increases the flow of urine and is thus helpful for cystitis and other urinary infections. It can be used to tone the heart and stimulate the circulation, and has been recommended for tension and emotional exhaustion. The French biochemist Madame Marguerite Maury wrote 'This essence creates a kind of euphoria; it interposes a padded zone between us and events.'

Benzoin is helpful for rheumatism, arthritis and gout. It is also useful for dry, cracked or reddened skin, particularly conditions such as dermatitis and eczema, and for fungal irritations of the skin as well as for problems such as melanosis when the skin becomes abnormally pigmented. Benzon is an excellent fixative and is widely used in perfume sachets and incense. It blends particulary well with rose and sandalwood.

Practical application

An excellent inhalation for colds and bronchitis can be made by adding a few drops of benzoin to 500 ml of water. For dry, chapped hands the oil can be mixed with glycerine and applied to the skin regularly. This ointment is very good for sore or cracked nipples of nursing mothers.

A soothing rub for aching joints and muscles can be made by adding one drop of benzoin to two teaspoons of almond oil.

BERGAMOT

Citrus bergamia

Bergamot oil comes from the rind of a citrus fruit and should not be confused with the herb bergamot, (*Monarda didyma*), also called wild bergamot or bee balm, which is a North American plant used to make herbal teas. This plant was so named because the scent of its leaves resembled that of bergamot oil.

Bergamot was first brought to Europe by Christopher Colombus who discovered it growing in the Canary Islands and it was named after the city of Bergamo in Lombardy where the essence was first sold. It is now grown in Italy, Sicily, southern France and along the Ivory Coast of Africa, but the main production area is in southern Italy.

The small tree, which resembles an orange or lemon tree, produces fragrant flowers and a pale yellow fruit which looks like a pear-shaped orange. The fruit is picked as soon as it is ripe, from December till February, and the outer part of the fresh peel is used to distill a yellowish-green oil with a spicy lemon scent. Five hundred grams of this oil can be produced from 100 kilos of fruit with the pulp of the fruit being used to make citric acid.

The oil contains 35–45 per cent linalyl acetate, limonene and linalol. It is antiseptic and antispasmodic, and is helpful for gastric and intestinal infections. Bergamot stimulates the appetite, aids digestion, eases flatulence and colic, as well as acting as a general tonic for the whole body. Its antiseptic qualities make it useful for the treatment of infections, particularly those of the skin, respiratory and urinary tracts. It can be used for eczema, acne, slow-healing wounds, parasitic conditions such as scabies, as well as for tonsilitis, bronchitis, tuberculosis, cystitis, leucorrhoea and vaginal pruritus.

Bergamot is also used to reduce fevers, especially intermittent ones. It has been used for this purpose by generations of Italian peasants who found it invaluable for expelling intestinal worms. Bergamot is an effective deodorant and can eliminate bad breath. The oil is used in sleep pillows and is a mild sedative, useful for the relief of anxiety and stress. Perhaps this is one of the reasons for the popularity of Earl Grey tea in which bergamot is used as a flavouring. The oil is added as a flavour to confectionery, pastries and medicines, and is widely used in the perfume industry for its warm, sweet scent with just a slight citrus tang.

Bergamot has an unusual reaction on the skin and actually increases its photosensitivity. For this reason it has been mixed with coconut oil and used in suntan oils designed to promote a rapid tan. However, it offers no protection against the sun's damaging ultra-violet rays and therefore should be used with caution and avoided by people in tropical climates, particularly those with a fair skin. It should never be applied in concentrated form to the skin as it can cause abnormal pigmentation.

Some therapists have used bergamot in the treatment of cancer, patients claiming that it helps to minimise the symptoms and side-effects.

Practical application

For colic and flatulence, especially in the small intestine, three drops of bergamot oil can be taken on sugar three times a day. If lack of appetite is a problem, this dose, taken half an hour before each meal, should rectify the situation.

A relaxing herbal pillow, guaranteed to promote a good night's restful sleep, can be made from rose buds mixed with rose and geranium leaves and sprinkled with a few drops of oil of bergamot, geranium rose and neroli.

CAJEPUT

Melaleuca leucadendron

Cajeput oil comes from a white tree of the same name which grows abundantly in Southeast Asia, especially Malaysia and the Molucca Islands, and is also found in the Philippines, Celebes and northern Australia. The English name comes from the Malay *kayu-puti* which means 'white tree' and it is also known as white tea-tree or swamp tea-tree.

Like the different species of melaleuca, often called paperbarks, which are common in more southern parts of Australia, *Melaleuca leucodendron* has a corky, layered bark which peels off in spongy sheets. The tribal Aborigines of northern Queensland drink a decoction of young leaves for headaches, colds and other illnesses.

The leaves and buds of the tree have a very strong aromatic smell and it is from these that cajeput oil is obtained by steam distillation. Its principal constituents are: cineol (60–75 per cent), d-pinene, terpineol and aldehydes.

The oil is a highly effective antiseptic, in fact one of the most powerful of all plant-derived germ killers. It is extremely useful for insect bites, wounds, scratches and infected sores. Cajeput can be used for infections of the pulmonary, intestinal and urinary tracts, including bronchitis, asthma, laryngitis, gastritis, dysentery and cystitis. Its analgesic qualities make it useful for migraine, flu, painful periods, rheumatism, aching muscles and toothache. It is also used for nervous vomiting, infant colic, to revive a person who is feeling faint, or it can calm one who is on the verge of hysterics. A few drops placed on the skin around the eyes will relieve eye strain and sunstroke. In Southeast Asian countries it is used to expel intestinal worms.

The oil of a closely-related species, *Melaleuca viridiflora*, which is particularly common in New Caledonia, is marketed as Niaouli or Gomenol. Its main ingredients are 35–66 per cent eucalyptol, 15 per cent terpinol, d-pinene, l-limonene, citrene, terebenthene, and valeric, acetic and butyric esters. Like cajeput, niaouli is an antiseptic, analgesic and vermifuge and is used in similar ways. It is particularly good for soothing inflammations of the ear, sinusitis and nasal catarrh.

Practical application

Cajeput oil can be applied full strength to external wounds, bites and infections or, if preferred, it can be diluted with olive oil.

An ointment made from three drops of cajeput and five teaspoons of soya oil makes a very soothing rub for rheumatism and other aches and pains.

An effective inhalation for colds and respiratory congestion can be made by adding three to four drops of cajeput oil to 500 ml of hot water.

For internal infections the oil can be taken in doses of two to five drops on brown sugar or honey, three or four times a day.

CAMPHOR

Cinnamomum camphora

For thousands of years camphor was only used in Asian countries. It was not known to the Greeks and Romans although there are records of its being used by Arabic peoples to lessen sexual desire. It is first mentioned in English herbals in the late seventeenth century.

Camphor is obtained from a large evergreen tree which is native to Japan, China and Formosa, but has been successfully introduced to other sub-tropical areas such as India, Australia and California. The tree, often called Camphor Laurel, grows up to 30 metres (100 ft) and has small shiny elliptical leaves, tiny white flowers and dark red berries. Camphor, with its characteristic pungent smell, is found throughout the tree but it takes many years to form. It is not present in commercial quantities until the tree is over fifty years old. It is extracted from the wood of the branches which are cut into chips and then boiled in water. The camphor rises to the surface and becomes solid as the water cools.

The clear, pungent-smelling oil extracted by steam distillation, is a ketone and is poisonous if swallowed.

Even inhaled in large quantities it can cause convulsions in people prone to epilepsy. Used externally, it is helpful for bruises, sprains, rheumatic and muscular pains as well as for headaches.

Camphor is a strong heart stimulant and can invigorate circulation and respiration as well as lower blood-pressure. In very small doses it is used to lower fevers, and help severe vomiting and diarrhoea. It is sometimes used in inhalations for coughs, bronchitis and other respiratory problems.

Perhaps its best-known use is as an insect repellent. For centuries chests and closets made of camphor wood have been used to store clothes away from the ravages of moths and other insects. In Southeast Asia it has also been used to preserve the bodies of the dead.

Because of potentially toxic effects of camphor, some therapists now prefer to use borneo camphor or borneol (*Dryobalanops camphora*). This oil is exuded from the wood of a tree native to Borneo and Sumatra and, unlike the more commonly known Japanese camphor, is an alcohol not a ketone and is not poisonous. The therapeutic powers of this oil have been known for thousands of years — in fact it was preserved by King Chrosroes II of Persia among the treasures of his palace in Babylon. It too is a powerful stimulant and anti-depressant. Borneol has much stronger antiseptic qualities than camphor, acts as a general tonic, and helps the body to fight a variety of infections.

Practical application

Japanese camphor should be used internally, only occasionally and in small doses. Externally it can be added to ointments used for slow-healing wounds, and to inhalants used to clear the head during respiratory disorders.

Borneo camphor can be taken internally for a variety of ailments including gastritis, diarrhoea, fevers, infectious diseases and general weakness of the heart.

A preparation can be made from 10 mg borneol added to 100 ml of 90 per cent alcohol and flavoured with lemon essence. About 25 drops of this can be added to a hot, sweetened lemon drink and taken twice a day between meals.

CHAMOMILE

Matricaria chamomilla (German, True Chamomile)
Anthemis nobilis (Roman, English Chamomile)

There are several different varieties of chamomile, a plant which has been known and valued for centuries for its medicinal qualities as well as its pleasant fragrance which made it a popular strewing herb. In ancient Egypt chamomile was considered a sacred flower and used both as an offering to the sun god Ra as well as to cure the diseases of the common people. Arab physicians considered wild chamomile a panacea. Some Germanic tribes also dedicated chamomile to their sun god Baldur while in Prussia wreaths of chamomile were hung in houses to protect the occupants from lightning and thunder.

All types of chamomile belong to the daisy family and have characteristic daisy-like flowers, and a strong smell, rather like apples. It was this smell which earned it its Greek name *kamai melon* (ground apple) which later gave rise to the English name chamomile.

Roman chamomile is a spreading feathery-leafed plant with small daisy-like flowers which have white petals and a yellow centre. In Eng-land it is popular as a lawn covering, a hardy, pleasant-smelling alternative to grass. Even Buckingham Palace has a trimmed chamomile lawn. During Tudor times turf seats were made out of earth covered with a dense mat of chamomile, and many a romantic poet relaxed on a chamomile bed inhaling the sweet scent of apples and composing a sonnet to his beloved.

German chamomile is a hardy self-seeding annual which grows 69–90 cm tall and bears masses of smaller flowers. It is this variety which is most often used to make chamomile tea — a soothing and relaxing drink which is especially popular for over-wrought children. Beatrix Potter tells us it was chamomile tea Mrs Rabbit gave to her son Peter to calm him after his narrow escape from Mr McGregor's shotgun.

Chamomile is grown mainly for its flowers which are best picked in the morning before the sun has drawn out the volatile essence which is later extracted by steam distillation. Interest in chamomile has been revived over the last few years since the discovery that the oil contains azulene, a blue crystalline substance with excellent anti-inflammatory properties. It is especially good for skin conditions, chronic gastritis, colitis and cystitis as well as certain kinds of asthma and is used in numerous pharmaceutical preparations.

Roman chamomile contains about 1 per cent essential oil while German chamomile has only 0.25 per cent but it is this oil which is richer in azulene. Both varieties produce a bitter tasting oil with a light, refreshing smell rather like apples and they can vary in colour from light greenish-blue to dark blue. Roman chamomile essence contains angelic and isobutyric ethers, a bitter principal, camphor, anthemene, sesquiterpenes, azulene and artemol. German chamomile essence contains mainly ethers of caprylic and monylic acids, a hydrocarbon and azulene.

Chamomile essence has a low toxicity and so is especially suitable for children. It is helpful for all kinds of inflammatory conditions and will soothe skin disorders such as acne, burns, stings and rashes. It is good for conjunctivitis, infants' teething problems, rheumatism and neuralgia. General aches and pains as well as more specific ones such as headache or earache will often respond to chamomile. It is suitable for all sorts of inflammations of the stomach, intestines and urino-genital system such as gastritis, diarrhoea, colitis, cystitis, urinary stones and liver disorders, and also for asthma and bronchitis. In Germany it is known as 'mother herb' because of its effectiveness for female complaints, particularly menstrual and menopausal difficulties.

The antispasmodic, sedative effect of chamomile is well-known and makes it suitable for conditions such as stress, tension headaches, anxiety, insomnia, convulsions and general irritability. The oil is used in herbal shampoos as it is said to lighten the hair and discourage hair loss.

Practical application

For rheumatism and other aches and pains, massage the body with five teaspoons of soya oil combined with two drops of chamomile essence and two drops of rosemary essence.

Skin irritations can be soothed by dabbing with cotton wool soaked in a lotion made of 100 ml olive oil, 10 g chamomile essence and 5–10 g Borneo camphor.

For internal inflammations chamomile can be taken in doses of two to four drops three times a day.

Migraine headaches can sometimes be helped by sucking a lump of sugar which has been soaked in four drops of chamomile essence.

23

CLOVE

Eugenia caryophyllata
Eugenia aromatica

Among the earliest spices mentioned in ancient Chinese writings were cloves which were used to sweeten the breath before an audience with the emperor. Cloves were known to the Greeks and Romans too, and they used them for medicinal purposes and imported them from the East through the Arab caravan routes.

Because the shape of a clove rather resembles that of a nail it was named after the Latin word *clavus*, meaning 'nail'.

During the fifeenth century the Portuguese navigator Vasco da Gama sailed to the islands of the East Indies (now Indonesia) where he discovered clove trees growing on the Molucca Islands. Trees have since been planted on other tropical islands, particularly Zanzibar which is now the best-known producer of cloves, actually growing seven-eighths of the world's total production of 10 000 tonnes of cloves each year.

The trees are evergreen, with light greyish leaves and brilliant red flowers. The buds of these flowers are harvested when they are light red, then dried on grass mats in the sun until they turn reddish-brown. A rich, volatile oil is extracted from these buds (called cloves) by steam distillation. Its main consituents are: 70–85 per cent eugenol, aceteugenol, methyl alcohol, methyl salicylate, furfurol, pinene, vanillin and caryophyllene. One tree yields approximately 7–10 kilograms of cloves each year, and the essence from these is equal to almost one fifth of the total weight of the cloves.

Cloves are well-known for their use as a culinary flavouring and also in perfumes and potpourris but they also have considerable medicinal qualities. Although not as widely used today, cloves were once considered a panacea.

Clove oil is an effective antiseptic, useful for infections of all kinds, from colds and flu to more specific contagious and infectious diseases such as measles and diphtheria. It is good for infected wounds, sores and parasitic skin conditions, and is so effective in killing bacteria that it is used to clean microscope slides.

At the beginning of this century essence of clove was sometimes used to disinfect operating theatres and the hands of surgeons and nurses.

An interesting side-effect of the Dutch attempt to destroy many of the clove trees in order to create scarcity and keep the price high, was an outbreak of infectious diseases. The inhabitants of the area had formerly used oranges stuck with cloves as a protection against contagion.

Clove is carminative and antispasmodic and acts as a general aid to digestion, useful for preventing flatulence, diarrhoea and intestinal spasm. It can also be used to get rid of intestinal worms.

Used externally it is a well-known remedy for toothache and makes a good mouthwash and breath sweetener. It is also a particularly effective insect repellent.

Clove essence is an ingredient in the eye ointment *koheul* used in some Arab countries and has also been used in Russia to treat corneal leucomas. In West Germany it was used recently to develop a new type of general anaesthetic. It is recommended to ease the pain of childbirth and is also considered helpful for some cases of rheumatism.

Practical application

A simple and effective solution for cleansing wounds and sores can be made from distilled water containing 2 per cent essence of cloves.

For toothache the oil can be applied directly to the affected tooth.

A very efficient and quite pleasant-smelling insect repellent can be made from an orange stuck with cloves. This will have the added benefit of keeping the air free of many bacteria which may spread infectious diseases.

CORIANDER

Coriandrum sativum

Coriander has been used for thousands of years in different cultures all over the world. It is mentioned in the Old Testament as one of the herbs of the Passover whose seeds were said to taste 'like wafers made with honey' (Exodus 16:31), and records show that it was grown in the Hanging Gardens of Babylon. The ancient Egyptians used coriander in funeral offerings and to make a kind of wine which was thought to bring happiness and sound sleep. They exported it to the Romans who used it as a meat preservative, and later introduced it to Britain. The Greeks considered coriander an aphrodisiac and used it in love potions, while the Chinese believed the seeds held the power of immortality.

Ancient magicians burned coriander seeds to drive out evil spirits and bring on hallucinations. Modern research has shown that in large quantities coriander does have narcotic effects. Perhaps it is because of this narcotic quality that the seeds are still used to make gin and form the centres for the popular children's sweet, rainbow balls.

The plant itself is a medium-sized annual with bright-green feathery leaves and umbels of pinky-white flowers. These flowers produce small, pale, fawn fruits usually incorrectly called seeds. It is often called Chinese parsley although the taste is much fresher and more pungent than ordinary parsley. Originally grown in southern Europe and Asia, it is now cultivated in temperate climates all over the world, and is especially common in India where it is used extensively in cooking.

Coriander fruit should be harvested by cutting off the flower heads just before the seeds are ready to drop. The seeds are then separated and crushed, and the essential oil is obtained by steam distillation. This oil contains up to 80 per cent coriandrol (an isomer of borneol), cineol, geraniol, pinene and terpinine. Its medicinal properties are similar to those of aniseed and caraway.

Coriander oil is antispasmodic and carminative. The widespread use of its seeds as a seasoning, especially for curries and indigestible vegetables such as cabbage, is probably partly due to these properties. It is an effective appetite stimulant and generally aids digestion, helping to prevent flatulence, colic, painful stomach spasms and headaches which result from poor digestion. It is sometimes recommended for patients suffering from anorexia nervosa.

Used externally, it can be helpful to ease the pain of rheumatism.

It is interesting to note that coriander is an important ingredient in a number of apéritifs and liqueurs including gin, brandy, ambrosia, Melissa cordial, Senna syrup and the Basque drink Izzana.

Practical application

To stimulate the appetite one drop of coriander essence can be taken on sugar half an hour before each meal. It is even more effective if combined with other essences, so a solution can be made of 10 ml each of coriander, lemon and caraway, and 20 ml of chamomile. This can be taken in a dose of two drops before each meal.

To ease the pain of indigestion two drops of coriander essence can be taken on sugar after each meal.

The pain of rheumatic joints can be soothed by rubbing them with olive oil to which 10 per cent coriander essence has been added. This same oil can be used to rub onto the stomach when one is suffering from indigestion.

CYPRESS

Cupressus sempervirens

Cypress trees were first brought from Asia to Mediterranean Europe by the Phoenicians who colonised the island of Cyprus which derived its name from the tree. Its generic name is derived from two Greek words, *kuo* (I produce) and *parises* (equal), referring to the symmetrical way most species of this genus grow.

In classical mythology the cypress is the emblem of the gods of the underworld. Its branches were placed outside the house of a dead person and carried by mourners in funeral processions. According to the Greeks, Cyparissus was so distressed when he accidentally killed a sacred stag belonging to his friend Apollo that he begged the gods to allow his grief to last forever. They granted his wish by changing him into a cypress tree, which has become the symbol of the immortal soul and eternal death.

Both the ancient Egyptians and the Chinese were aware of the medicinal qualities of cypress, particularly for respiratory disorders, and the Chinese considered the nuts to be a nutritious and fattening food.

The tree itself is a tall, conical-shaped perennial, often found in European parks and gardens. The small flowers are followed by round greyish-brown cones called nuts. The nuts as well as the leaves contain an essential oil which is obtained by steam distillation. Its main constituents are: d-pinene, d-campene, d-sylvestrene, cymene, a ketone, sabinol, a terpenic alcohol, valeric acid and camphor of cypress.

Cypress oil is a powerful astringent; it helps stop bleeding and is useful in relieving circulatory problems such as haemorrhoids and varicose veins, and to treat oily skin. It is antispasmodic, useful for asthma and convulsive coughs and it also acts as a sedative on the nerve endings of the respiratory system, making it useful for bronchitis and flu. Problems associated with menstruation and menopause can often be alleviated by cypress oil and it is also good for overcoming incontinence and bedwetting. Used externally, cypress oil can reduce excessive sweating and the unpleasant odours associated with this, especially round the feet.

It can also be used to ease the pain of rheumatism.

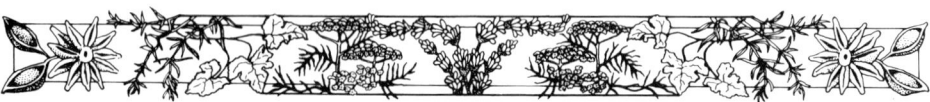

Practical application

For varicose veins and haemorrhoids add four to six drops of cypress essence to warm bath water. The legs can also be massaged with two to four drops of cypress oil in two teaspoons of soya oil.

To control bleeding from cuts and wounds, gently wash them in lukewarm water containing 1 per cent cypress oil.

For influenza and bronchitis, three drops of essence can be taken on brown sugar three times a day. The chest can also be rubbed with warm olive oil containing 10 per cent cypress oil. If a few drops of cypress oil are placed on the pillow they make an effective inhalant.

EUCALYPTUS

Eucalyptus globulus

There are over 300 different species of the eucalyptus tree in the world. Originally found only in Australia but, largely due to the work of the German botanist Baron Ferdinand von Muller (who was director of Melbourne Botanical Gardens from 1857–73), it is now grown in subtropical areas all over the world, particularly in Spain, Egypt, South Africa, India and California.

The eucalyptus, popularly known as the gum tree, has been used medicinally by Aborigines for thousands of years. The early white settlers were astounded by its healing properties and, in the absence of more orthodox medicines, used it to cure almost anything. Early Australian folklore abounds with tales of miraculous recoveries which were due to the effects of eucalyptus oil.

The name eucalyptus comes from the Greek *eucalyptos* meaning 'well covered', and is so named because the flower buds are covered with a cup-like membrane which is cast off as the flower grows. Unlike the leaves on many European trees, the tough grey-green leaves of the gum tree usually hang downwards, thus minimising their exposure to the hot sun and this minimises the evaporation of the essential oil and moisture.

About 50 species of gum are now cultivated for their essential oil. Those rich in eucalyptol (containing between 55 and 85 per cent) are used for medicine while the others are used in perfumes. The blue gum or *Eucalyptus globulus* is still the best-known and most widely-used. It produces a clear oil which is extracted by steam distillation. Its main constituents are: eucalyptol (80–85 per cent), phellandrene, aromadendrene, eudesmol, pinene, camphene, valeric, butyric and caproic aldehydes, ethyl and amylalcohols.

Eucalyptus is a very strong antiseptic. It is interesting to note that eucalyptus essence actually has greater antiseptic powers than pure eucalyptol. This is thought to be due to the effects of the small quantity of ozone which is produced by the oxidation of the phellandrenes and aromadrenes.

Eucalyptus oil can be used externally for all kinds of wounds, sores, cuts, parasitic skin infections, burns and insect bites, and also acts as an insect repellent. It makes an excellent fumigant to prevent the spread of infection as studies have shown that spraying with an emulsion containing 2 per cent eucalyptus oil will kill off 70 per cent of staphylococci in the air.

Internally it is useful for infections of all sorts, particularly those of the respiratory and urinary systems. It is an effective expectorant, particularly good for clearing up heavy mucus discharge associated with chest and throat infections, and is wonderful for opening the stuffed nasal passages of sinusitis sufferers.

Eucalyptus has a cooling effect on the body, it reduces high temperatures, and so is useful for all sorts of fevers. Its antiseptic and diuretic qualities are good for urino-genital infections such as cystitis and leucorrhoea, and it can also be used for cases of acute diarrhoea with mucus. Slow healing wounds and any kind of sepsis or toxaemia will generally respond to eucalyptus oil and it can also be rubbed into the skin to ease

muscular aches and pains and rheumatoid arthritis.

Practical application

An excellent inhalant for colds, bronchitis or sinusitis can be made by mixing 4 g eucalyptus oil, 2 g pine oil, 2 g thyme oil and 1 g lavender oil with 150 cc of 90 per cent alcoholic solution. A large spoonful of this mixture should be placed in a bowl of boiling water and inhaled, preferably with a towel draped over the head, two or three times a day for a week of more until the infection is gone.

A useful lotion for use as an insect repellent can be made by combining 30 g eucalyptus essence, 30 g lemon grass essence and 10 g thyme essence in a litre of 90 per cent alcohol. To ease the pain of rheumatism the affected joints should be rubbed with warm olive oil to which 100 g camphor and 60 g eucalyptus oil have been added.

EVENING PRIMROSE

Oenothera biennis

Often dismissed as a 'humble plant' because it is basically a weed, evening primrose is nevertheless very special indeed — its seeds are rich in polyunsaturated oils which help lower blood cholesterol and are useful in treating degenerative diseases.

The evening primrose was first described by English herbalist John Parkinson in 1629, and quickly established itself as a useful medicinal plant. According to Parkinson's contemporary, Nicholas Culpeper, it was useful as a diuretic and to treat 'obstructions of the liver and spleen'. Today, herbalists use the leaves and bark of the evening primrose for their astringent and sedative properties. However, the revival of interest in the plant is due not so much to its capacity as a herb as to the unique properties of its seed oil.

The evening primrose has golden yellow petals which open in the evening sun and die after a single evening. When the petals fall, numerous pods form on each stem and each pod contains tiny seeds — each similar in size to mustard seed. It is the oil extracted from these seeds which has special nutritional significance.

Evening primrose seeds were first analysed in 1917 and found to contain 15 per cent oil. Two years later a group of chemists discovered that the oil of the evening primrose was unique in its chemical composition — containing not only oleic and linoleic acids but a comparatively rare polyunsaturated acid called gamma-linolenic acid.

Much later, in the 1960s, when English scientists began to search for natural substances that could be used to treat heart disease, they found references in the literature to the unique composition of evening primrose seed oil. The fact that the oil contained approximately 72 per cent linoleic acid and 9 per cent gamma-linolenic acid (GLA) made the oil the most polyunsaturated oil available.

Gamma-linolenic acid is now known to lower blood cholesterol and is therefore extremely useful in the prevention of heart disease. Both linoleic and gamma-linolenic acid are classified as 'essential fatty acids' — vitamin-like constituents which are vital for cell and body function but which cannot be made by the body itself. They resemble, and complement, naturally occurring prostaglandins in the body which regulate blood pressure, increase blood flow to the organs and help reduce blood clots. The fact that evening primrose seeds were found to be so rich in these essential fatty acids was a discovery of some importance.

Dr David Horrobin, Professor of Medicine at the University of Montreal, was so intrigued by the health-potential of evening primrose oil that in 1981 he gave up his academic post to devote himself to full-time research on the oil. He has since confirmed clinically that the oil is able to lower blood cholesterol levels, reduce blood pressure, inhibit thrombosis, control arthritis, treat eczema, decrease hyperactivity in children, and assist alcoholism.

Meanwhile, Dr Kenneth Vaddadi, a psychiatrist at the University of Leeds, has successfully used gamma-linolenic acid to treat schizophrenic patients. He now believes that schizophrenia may be caused by a disturbance in prostaglandin function and, as we have seen, these prostaglandins closely resemble gamma-linolenic acid in composition.

There could also be new hope for those suffering from multiple sclerosis. These people usually have a deficiency of linoleic acid in their blood, and since evening primrose oil is especially rich in this constituent, the oil is now being used in the treatment of this condition.

So, linoleic and gamma-linolenic acids could prove to be among the most significant nutrients yet discovered — perhaps as important as Vitamin C. And the evening primrose — the 'humble plant' of the medieval herbalists — has emerged as the richest natural source of these vital substances.

Practical application

General use to help prevent heart disease take up to six 500 mg capsules per day.

For schizophrenia take six to eight 500 mg capsules per day in conjunction with Vitamin B_3 (7.5 mg); Vitamin B_6 (25 mg); Vitamin C (125 mg) and Zinc (2.5 mg). (Dose recommended by the Schizophrenia Association of Great Britain.)

FENNEL

Foeniculum vulgare

Tales of fennel's wondrous magical properties have formed part of the folklore in China, India, Egypt and Greece. According to Greek mythology Prometheus hid the fire of the sun in a hollow fennel stalk when he first carried it down from heaven to earth. The Roman scholar Pliny believed that fennel enabled the eye to see the beauty of nature with clarity, and it soon gained a reputation for its ability to improve eyesight. Greek athletes are said to have eaten fennel when competing in the Olympic Games because they believed it strengthened their muscles without making them fat. In England bunches of fennel were hung up to keep away evil spirits and witches, and fennel seeds were stuffed into the keyholes to keep ghosts out of the house. The herbalist Culpeper recommended fennel as an antidote to poisonous plants and snakebite.

Native to the Mediterranean regions of Europe, fennel is now cultivated and also grows wild in temperate climates all over the world. It is a tall, hardy perennial with delicate bright-green feathery leaves and umbels of yellow flowers which produce clusters of seeds. Both the leaves and seeds have an aniseed taste.

The essential oil is obtained by steam distillation of the pulverised seeds. Its principal constituents are: 50–60 per cent anethol, fenchone, estragol, camphene and phellandrene.

Fennel is used mainly as a digestive aid — to stimulate the appetite and prevent colic, flatulence, nausea, constipation and even hiccups. It is also a diuretic and can be helpful for kidney complaints, obesity and fluid retention. Fennel oil can be used to increase the milk supply of nursing mothers, for scanty periods and for menopausal problems.

Anethol, the principal ingredient of fennel, has been shown to reduce the toxic effects of alcohol on the body.

Fennel oil can also be used for bronchitis, to stop the spasmodic coughing in whooping cough and to help prevent colds and flu. It expels intestinal worms. Externally it can be used to strengthen the gums and to improve deafness and weak eyesight.

Practical application

A few fennel seeds chewed daily will guard against winter colds and flu, and help prevent indigestion and bad breath. If preferred, indigestion, especially flatulence, can also be helped by taking two drops of fennel essence on a lump of sugar after each meal.

GARLIC

Allium sativum

Garlic is a remarkable herb with an exotic history. According to Herodotus, the builders of the Great Pyramid in Egypt were issued with a clove of garlic each day as a tonic, and preserved garlic bulbs have also been recovered from the tomb of Tutankhamen. It is also mentioned several times by Homer, Virgil and Horace as a popular panacea in ancient Greece and Rome. For example, Hippocrates recommended it for indigestion and bowel complaints. In ancient China, on the other hand, it was used to ease skin problems and circulatory disorders that required treatment classified as 'hot and dry'.

Garlic is a perennial plant and grows in well-drained soil to a height of 90 cm. Its slender green leaves are around 30 cm in length and from the centre of the plant a stalk emerges which bears a small, mauve-white flower. However, it is the bulb which is of most interest to us here, for it is this part of the plant which has medicinal value.

The mature bulb consists of a cluster of cloves, each cased in a type of papery covering. Garlic cloves contain Vitamins A, B_1, B_2 and C, minerals such as copper, manganese, iron, calcium and sulphur, and in particular, a unique amino acid called alliin. When garlic is crushed, this converts to a substance called allicin, which has a distinct aroma and taste. It is the allicin component of garlic which is effective against infections, and garlic is a wonderful natural antiseptic. The sulphides in allicin also work to lower cholesterol levels in the body and have a pronounced anti-clotting effect.

Natural odourless garlic oil can be taken in capsules if you wish to avoid the smell of garlic on your breath! Not all forms of odourless garlic have active allicin content, however, and it may be necessary to research the products available in your health shop. Arizona Natural Odourless Garlic, for example, has been classified as containing allicin in an independent laboratory analysis using the Boeringer-Mannheim method.

Practical application

Garlic oil is an excellent supplement for aiding hay-fever and sinus prob-

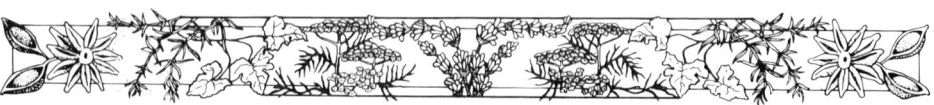

lems and can be taken to treat blemishes and pimples. Here it works from the inside, restoring the skin to good health in a few days. Garlic oil is also suitable for throat and vaginal infections and acts as a cleanser for the intestines. In this last capacity it serves as an anthelmintic to expel worms. Garlic oil may also be applied externally to parts of the body affected by rheumatism and along the spine to treat general weakness and debility.

You can make your own garlic oil for external use by mixing 100 g of crushed garlic with 200 g olive oil and 10 g of camphor — then allowing the mixture to macerate for two weeks prior to straining. However, for internal use it may be preferable to purchase garlic capsules from your health shop and take as prescribed — at least this way the allicin content can be guaranteed.

GERANIUM

Pelargonium odorantissimum

There are over 700 different species of geranium which can be divided into more than 20 genera. One of these, Herb Robert, (*Geranium robertianum*), which is a common British variety, has certain qualities similar to *Pelargonium odorantissimum*.

Geraniums originated in Africa. According to Muslim legend the first specimen appeared when the prophet Mohammed, having washed his shirt, hung it on a bush to dry and turned aside to say his prayers. When he had finished praying he removed his shirt and found the bush had transformed into a geranium.

Geranium oil was regarded by ancient civilisations as an excellent substance to mend fractures and cure cancers. It was first introduced to Europe towards the end of the seventeenth century and is now widely used in perfumery. The common garden plants known as geraniums were developed in the eighteenth century by crossing different varieties of pelargonia. The particular type known as *Pelargonium odorantissimum* is an aromatic plant with small pink flowers and serrated pointed leaves. It is found growing wild on wasteland and at the edge of forests. The whole plant can be used in infusion or the essential oil can be obtained by steam distillation of the green parts, especially the leaves. It is a sweet scented oil, clear or light green in colour and with a bitter taste. Its main constituents are geraniol, citronellol, linalol, terpineol and alcohol.

Geranium oil is of great value in skin care. It is cleansing, refreshing, astringent and useful for all sorts of skin inflammations, including dermatitis, dry eczema, ringworm, excessive oiliness and even burns and wounds. Additionally it is helpful for haemorrhoids and bad circulation and makes a very relaxing and refreshing bath oil which can often relieve the pain of neuralgia as it is a mild sedative and analgesic.

Geranium oil is an excellent insect repellent because of its terpene content. It is a mild antiseptic and can be useful for sore throats and to disinfect wounds. It is also a mild diuretic which can be used for fluid retention and urinary tract disorders. Some therapists recommend it for diarrhoea and gastroenteritis.

Essence of geranium stimulates the adrenal cortex which controls hormones which in turn regulate and balance the functions of the body. It is often helpful for correcting hormonal imbalance especially during menopause. Many nursing mothers find geranium oil particularly helpful for treating painful, engorged or congested breasts.

An Italian scientist, Dr Simone Vetrano, has discovered the presence of an anti-coagulant substance in the leaves of many species of pelargonia, particularly the ornamental ones. This may be of great importance in controlling haemorrhages.

Practical application

Painful inflammations of the breasts can be eased by applying about three drops of geranium oil mixed with cold cream. In addition, the breasts should be bathed regularly with a solution of fresh water containing 2 g geranium oil per litre.

Inflamed skin can first be washed with pure water containing 2 per cent geranium oil, then smeared with olive oil which has been combined with 10 per cent essence of geranium. A soothing massage oil for aching muscles and joints can be made from 2–3 drops of geranium oil in two teaspoons of soya oil.

HYSSOP

Hyssopus officinalis

Hyssop is an aromatic herb which has been used for over 2000 years both as a culinary seasoning and for medicinal purposes. Some people believe the name is of Greek origin, derived from the name of a holy herb *azob* while others believe our modern hyssop is in fact the plant known to the ancient Hebrews as *ezob* and mentioned in Psalm 51 verse 9; 'Purge me with hyssop and I shall be clean'. Perhaps because of its deodorant properties, it was one of the herbs used to purify sacred temples, and the Hebrews used bunches of it for the ritual cleansing of lepers. Hippocrates used hyssop to treat pleurisy. In early Christian tradition hyssop was symbolic of baptism and renewed innocence while mythologically it has been coupled with cedar to typify the yearly cycle of the sun passing through the winter solstice to summer and back again.

The plant itself is indigenous to southern Europe and northern Asia, but is now grown in other parts of the world — in Britain it can sometimes be found growing wild, round the walls of old Cistercian monasteries.

Hyssop is a medium-sized shrubby herb with slender dark green leaves and usually blue flowers, though some varieties can be pink or white. It grows best in warm dry places, often on sunny hillsides.

The leaves are strongly aromatic and contain a volatile oil which is obtained by distillation. Its main constituents are borneol, phillandrene, geraniol, limonene, thujone and pinocamphene. Pinocamphene is a ketone which is toxic in high doses and may cause epileptic fits. Most of the healing qualities of hyssop can also be found in an infusion of the leaves and because this is not so potent, some practitioners prefer to use it.

As Hippocrates discovered, hyssop is an expectorant, useful for bronchitis, coughs and chest congestion as it loosens mucus and also acts as a mild relaxing sedative which can relieve bronchial spasms and asthma. It has a regulating effect on the circulatory system and can be useful for hypertension. Hyssop helps the digestion, particularly of meat fats, and can be taken to stimulate the appetite and reduce flatulence and mild constipation. Sometimes it is recommended for kidney stones and for menstrual problems and leucorrhoea. The oil will kill intestinal worms and used externally it will kill head lice. Its antiseptic qualities make it useful as a gargle for sore throats and a wash for eczema, wounds and sores. Some people have suggested that hyssop is helpful in fighting cancer but this has yet to be proved.

Hyssop oil is used in expensive perfumes, colognes and liqueurs — it is an important ingredient of Chartreuse. The smell has been described as a mixture of basil, geranium and thyme.

Practical application

For a sore throat, three drops of essence can be taken with brown sugar or honey three times a day. In addition a lukewarm gargle should be made from a mixture of 100 mls of boiled water and a teaspoon of alcoholic preparation containing 5 per cent hyssop essence. This should be used frequently.

For chronic bronchitis take three drops of essence in honey three times a day. Additionally, the whole chest area should be rubbed each night with a cream made from 1000 g sweet almond oil, 250 g white wax, 750 g distilled water and 25 g hyssop essence.

JOJOBA

Simmondsia chinensis

Jojoba (pronounced ho-ho-ba) is a unique plant. The golden oil, or wax, extracted from its seed pod has many uses as a cosmetic oil and, remarkably enough, is also a possible commercial substitute for sperm whale oil.

Quite apart from its potential as an alternative to sperm whale oil — these whales have been protected in the United States since 1970 by the Endangered Species Conservation Act — jojoba is a traditional healing plant with very distinctive characteristics. Jojoba oil resembles spermaceti wax, has excellent lubricating qualities, and is a fine moisturiser for the skin.

Jojoba evolved in northern Mexico and the south-western region of the United States, and has been known variously as 'Deer Nut', 'Wild Hazel', 'Coffee Berry' and 'Goat Nut'. Originally classified by the English botanist H.F. Link, who discovered a specimen growing near San Diego in the 1840s, jojoba was already known to the Cahuilla Indians of southern California, who made a drink from it. The Seri Indians used its oil to relieve inflamed eyes, colds and sore throats. Later, the Spanish-speaking Mexicans also began to grind the seeds to make a beverage comparable to cocoa, and Mexican males were fond of using the oil to promote the growth of their eyebrows and moustaches!

As a plant, jojoba hasn't a particularly distinctive appearance. Its leaves are grey-green, it grows to around two metres in height, and its rate of growth is slow — it may take five years to reach maturity. Jojoba has a small, brown, nut-like fruit and favours coarse, well-drained desert soils. The seed in the pod ripens during the summer and in autumn falls to the ground or becomes entangled in its own luxuriant growth. It is this seed — which resembles a large coffee bean in size — that contains the distinctive golden oil.

The oil, or wax, in the jojoba seed is unusual. Whereas other plants produce their oils by combining glycerol and fatty acids, jojoba combines fatty alcohols with fatty acids to produce an oil which does not oxidise and therefore will not become rancid. This means it has an extremely long shelf-life. Jojoba also contains an anti-inflammatory agent known as myristic acid.

Jojoba's unique chemical composition makes it suitable for use in wood polishes and floor waxes, candles, and also as a machine lubricant. It can also be used for cooking and can serve as a nutty-tasting salad dressing. However, it is its healing and moisturising properties which are of most interest to us here.

Pure cold-pressed jojoba oil may be applied to all types of skin, and can be used to treat such conditions as dry scalp, psoriasis and eczema. If applied lightly, it can act as a fine facial moisturiser, and its penetrating qualities help to soften the skin. Jojoba also conditions the hair and it is a familiar ingredient in many commercial soaps and shampoos.

Practical application

Apply a few drops of jojoba oil directly to chapped or sore lips, dry skin, or general skin disorders like eczema, dandruff, psoriasis or acne. It is also surprisingly effective in treating persistent warts. As one might expect, jojoba oil is valuable in the heat of summer: it does not actually prevent sunburn but helps the skin to retain its moisture, and may be used in conjunction with other skin-care cosmetics and sun-blocking creams.

A few ground and roasted jojoba beans may be eaten each morning to strengthen a weak stomach and relieve acidity — indeed, this was a traditional Mexican remedy — but the amount taken should not be excessive: larger quantities may have a purgative effect.

Because jojoba contains anti-inflammatory myristic acid it also has potential value to relieve arthritis and rheumatism, and can be rubbed directly into sore joints.

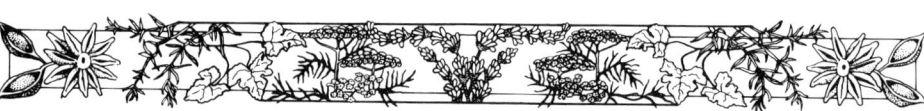

JUNIPER

Juniperus communis

The magical powers of juniper berries have formed part of the legends and folklore of many countries of the world. Some believe it was a juniper bush which shielded the Virgin Mary and her baby Jesus from Herod's soldiers as they fled to Egypt. In medieval times the berries were burned at funerals to keep away less tangible enemies — the ghosts and evil spirits which might be lurking nearby. The green branches were burned to smoke out witches and drive off dark forces, while in Wales the tree was regarded as sacred, and its destruction likely to cause a death in the family. In more practical Switzerland the branches were burnt in school rooms and hospitals to disinfect them when it was too cold to open the windows.

Juniper is a hardy shrub or small tree which grows in Europe, North America and Asia. It has reddish stems with needle-like leaves and a strong smell, rather like pine. The small yellow flowers bloom in early summer and, if a male tree is planted nearby, the female will produce green berries which gradually ripen over three years until they turn blue and then finally black. Each of these berries contains three seeds. The ripe berries, gathered in autumn, can be crushed to produce juniper oil, a colourless or pale yellow liquid which becomes darker and thicker with age. This oil is rich in alphapinene, cadinene, camphene, terpineol, terpenic alcohol, borneol, isoborneol and camphor of juniper. It is well-known for its use in distilling gin and as a flavouring for meats, but it has also been used medicinally for hundreds of years.

Juniper stimulates the appetite — an excuse perhaps for a pre-dinner gin — and is an excellent remedy for colic, flatulence and all kinds of digestive disorders. It is an extremely effective diuretic, often used for cystitis and kidney stones, and to relieve fluid retention and gout as well as for rheumatism and arthritis. Because of its antiseptic properties it is good for many internal infections — of the urinary tract, intestines, chest and blood, and it will also stimulate blood circulation. It can be used for painful menstruation, scanty periods and leucorrhoea and its sedative qualities help in the relief of nervous tension, anxiety and sleeplessness or as a general tonic for those leading a particularly stressful life.

Used externally, juniper's anti-septic and astringent properties help eczema, dermatitis, haemorrhoids, acne and most sorts of skin disorders and it makes a good aromatic water for cleansing and toning the skin, particularly if it is oily. Juniper berries can also be used for diabetes.

Practical application

For troublesome acne, the skin should be smeared with olive oil containing 10 per cent juniper essence. This same oil can be rubbed onto the lower abdomen to treat cystitis. At the same time the patient should take four drops of juniper essence on a little brown sugar after every meal.

Instead of swallowing the essence in concentrated form, some people prefer to make juniper wine which can be taken a glassful at a time as an apéritif before the evening meal. One recipe for this is to add one litre of white wine to 30 g crushed juniper berries and 15 g chopped stalks. Leave to steep for four days before straining and add up to 30 g sugar if desired.

LAVENDER

Lavandula officinalis
Lavandula dentata

The English word 'lavender' originally comes from the Latin verb *lavo*, 'I wash', and for centuries lavender has been used for soaps and bath water. Its pleasant scent has made it a favourite perfume and one which has been associated especially with English ladies. Although lavender was traditionally given by lovers as a sign of affection, it was also believed that lavender water sprinkled over a maiden's head would help to preserve her chastity and that a thriving lavender plant in the garden was an indication that the daughter of the house would never marry, thus fulfilling the saying 'Lavender will only grow in old maids' gardens'.

There are a number of different varieties of lavender, the best-known being English lavender (*Lavandula officinalis* or *Lavandula spica*) and French lavender (*Lavandula dentata*) which has a slightly less potent perfume but, with denser and more attractive flowering heads, is often preferred by gardeners. The leaves of both varieties are slender and silvery-green, and the flowers nearly always mauve although they can be white.

All lavenders are native to the Mediterranean region but have now been introduced to many other parts of the world. There is no record of lavender being cultivated in England before about 1568, although as it was a favourite plant of the Greeks and Romans it is quite possible that the Romans took some with them when they settled in England.

Lavender flowers should be picked before the last flowers on the stalk have opened, for it is then that their oil content is highest. Harvesting should be done in the morning of a dry day so that the sun has not had time to draw out the volatile essence which can then be extracted by steam distillation. Its main constituents are ethers of linalyl and geranyl, geraniol, linalol, cineol, d-borneol, limonene, l-pinene, caryophyllene, butyric and valeric esters and coumarin. The exact amount of these different substances varies according to the type of lavender and the climate in which it is grown, but on average 200 kilos of flowers will yield 750–1000 g of essence.

Lavender has a tranquillising effect — this can be experienced merely by picking the flowers and inhaling their scent. The oil calms the nerves, relaxes tension and has a similar reviving effect to smelling salts. It has been widely used for centuries to relieve feelings of faintness, dizziness, headache, nervous palpitations and insomnia. Lavender is antispasmodic and can be helpful for asthma, bronchitis and nausea, dyspepsia, infant colic or other gastric complaints which may be associated with nervous and emotional problems. Some herbalists recommend a soothing rub of lavender oil for rheumatism and arthritis.

Practical application

For migraine and other headaches, three drops of essence can be taken on a little brown sugar after every meal. The effect of this is enhanced if cool compresses are held on both the forehead and neck. These should be made from 1000 ml of a solution which is 80 per cent alcohol and has been mixed with 100 g Borneo camphor, 40 ml essence of lavender and 20 ml essence of aspic.

For acne and other troublesome skin conditions, the face should be washed with lavender water containing 2 per cent of lavender essence, then smoothed with a cream made from 1000 g sweet almond oil, 250 g white wax, 750 g distilled water, 20 g essence of lavender and 5 g aspic.

Individual sores or insect bites can be dabbed directly with essence of lavender.

LEMON

Citrus limonum

This very popular citrus fruit is thought to have originated in India. It was probably first brought to Europe from Media, an ancient region south-west of the Caspian Sea in what is now the USSR. For some time it was known as the Median apple and has been depicted in some Christian art as being the fruit of the Tree of Knowledge of Good and Evil which was eaten by Eve in the Garden of Eden.

Lemon trees now thrive in sunny, temperate or sub-tropical climates all over the world, and grow particularly well in places like Spain and California. They need light, fairly sandy soil with good drainage and will often bear a prolific crop for many years.

Lemon essence is extracted by pressing the outer part of the fresh rind or pericarp. The lemon contains numerous large pockets of essence in the sub-epidermic parenchyma. Green fruits have more essence than ripe ones but, nevertheless, more than 3000 lemons are needed to produce one kilo of essence. The pulp which is left over from these lemons is used to make citric acid. It is about 30 per cent juice (which contains

6–8 per cent citric acid) as well as glucides, mineral salts, gums and vitamins, especially vitamin C (up to 50 mg per 100 g of fruit). The lemon essence itself is made up of approximately 95 per cent terpenes (pinene, limonene, phellandrene, camphene, sesquiterpenes), linalol, acetates of linalyl and geranyl, citral and citronella (six–eight per cent), aldehydes and camphor of lemon.

Lemon is well-known as a flavouring used in a variety of drinks, desserts and savoury dishes, and the oil is used in perfumes and to flavour unpleasant medicines. All parts of the lemon have useful medicinal qualities. Lemon juice is a well-tried home remedy for a number of ailments, particularly colds and sore throats, and can also be used externally to stop bleeding wounds, as a hair rinse and facial astringent, to soothe sunburn, fade freckles and soften warts and corns.

Lemon essence is a powerful antibacterial agent. It can be diluted with water and used as a gargle for sore throats, and thrush, and as a wash to clean sores and wounds, and to stop bleeding. It can be applied

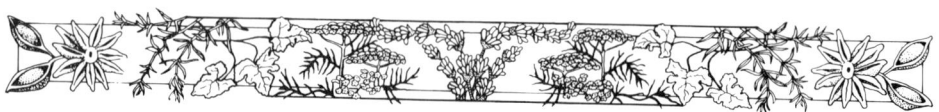

directly to insect stings and warts. Research has shown that lemon essence neutralises staphylococcus, tuberculosis bacillus, Eberth's bacillus and Loefflers bacillus in a matter of minutes. A few drops will kill 92 per cent of all bacteria in oysters within fifteen minutes.

Some aromatherapists recommend a dose of three drops of lemon essence on brown sugar four times a day to fight infectious diseases. Lemon essence is sometimes recommended for liver complaints and to regulate stomach acidity. It also has diuretic and laxative properties. As well as acting as a heart tonic, it stimulates the white corpuscles and also helps to stop bleeding. It is sometimes recommended for arteriosclerosis and hypertension.

Practical application

For chest conditions such as asthma and bronchitis, five drops of lemon essence can be taken on brown sugar three times a day. The treatment becomes more effective if the patient occasionally takes deep breaths from a bottle of essence and has a chest and back massage with warm olive oil which has been mixed with 10 per cent lemon essence. This oil can also be used to rub on rheumatic joints. The patient can take a smaller dose of 3 drops of essence after each meal.

Facial wrinkles can be smoothed with a cream made from 1000 g sweet almond oil, 250 g white wax, 30 g tincture of benzoin, 750 g distilled water and 20 g essence of lemon. Brittle nails can often be strengthened by immersing them for 15 minutes each night in warm olive oil to which 10 per cent essence of lemon has been added. Lemon essence can be added to strengthen the healing properties of any preparation made from lemon juice.

MARJORAM (SWEET, KNOTTED MARJORAM)

Origanum marjorana

This familiar culinary herb was originally found in Mediterranean, North African and Middle Eastern countries and was known and used by the ancient Egyptians as well as the Greeks and Romans who introduced it to Britain at the time of their conquest. It is one of the sacred herbs of India, dedicated to the gods Shiva and Vishnu. The generic name, which loosely translated means 'joy of the mountains', comes from two Greek words. Marjoram was used for medicinal purposes as well as for perfumes and toiletries. It was a popular strewing herb used to give houses a clean, pleasant smell and to freshen linen cupboards.

In Greece sweet marjoram is sometimes called *amarakos* after a Greek myth which tells of a young man named Amarakos who was a servant in the household of King Cinyrus of Cyprus. One day, in the course of his duties, he dropped a jar of perfume and was so apprehensive about the king's reaction that he fainted. The gods are said to have taken pity on him and turned him into a marjoram plant to protect him from the king's wrath.

The Greeks regarded marjoram as a symbol of happiness and wellbeing, and used it in wedding garlands. They considered that a marjoram plant growing over a grave was a sign that the dead person beneath was sure to be content and at peace.

Marjoram is a bushy, low-growing plant with small soft grey-green leaves and clusters of tiny white flowers which grow at the tips of the stems. It should be harvested in summer just before the plant is in full-flower. The essential oil is extracted from the whole plant by stem distillation. It is colourless, bitter-tasting and has a strong, persistent odour. The principal ingredients are: camphor and borneol (which together make up 85 per cent) and various terpenes including terpineol, sabinene, pinene and origanol. It is interesting to note that the plant's content of essential oil will increase if stinging nettles are growing nearby.

Marjoram oil is an anti-spasmodic which soothes indigestion and flatulence caused by intestinal spasms. It has a sedative and tonic action on the nervous system and is helpful for insomnia, general anxiety, high blood pressure and some migraine headaches. It acts as a general vasodilator on the autonomic nervous system. For headcolds, catarrh and the headaches often associated with them, it can be used either as an inhalant or as an oil with which to massage the temples and sinus areas. Marjoram oil is often helpful for leucorrhoea and painful menstruation. It is an excellent warming and relaxing oil to add to the bath water which will ease muscular pains, fatigue and strain. It makes a very effective rub for rheumatism, sprains and muscular cramps and also helps to disperse bruises and ease the discomfort of varicose veins.

Marjoram is said to be an anaphrodisiac useful for curbing excessive sexual desires and obsessive masturbation. This quality was apparently first discovered by a clergyman who ran a home for orphans. Marjoram oil makes a good, though rather expensive, furniture polish, and is sometimes used to darken and enrich the colour of brown hair.

Practical application

For high blood pressure, five drops of marjoram oil should be taken on a little sugar between meals.

Insomnia and general anxiety can often be relieved by taking three drops of essence with honey about half an hour before bedtime.

Migraine headaches can often be eased by rubbing the forehead, temples and the back of the neck with an alcoholic solution made from one litre of 80 per cent alcohol mixed with 100 g borneol and 60 g marjoram essence.

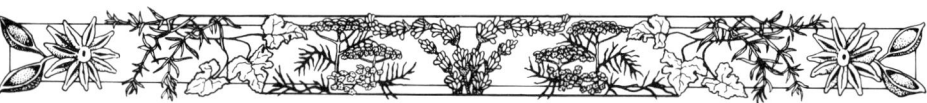

NUTMEG

Myristica fragrans

Mace and nutmeg, both of which come from the fruit of the nutmeg tree, have been known and used for thousands of years. Traces of nutmeg have been found in the remains of Egyptian mummies and the Roman scholar Pliny, in the first century AD, described this unusual tree with a fragrant nut and two kinds of perfume. From the sixth century Arabs imported large quantities of mace and nutmeg, and later introduced them to the Europeans. By the fourteenth century mace was one of the most expensive and highly-prized of the oriental spices used in England.

The tree grows in hot, steamy, tropical islands and it is sometimes said that the birds who live in a forest of such trees become intoxicated by the aromatic fumes. It is native to Indonesia and is also grown in parts of the West Indies and Sri Lanka.

The slow-growing tree does not bear fruit for the first seven years, and eventually grows to a height of about eight metres. The trees are either male or female but only one male tree is needed to fertilise twenty female trees. When ripe, the large fleshy fruit splits open to reveal a glossy brown kernel about three centimetres long and two centimetres wide which is wrapped in a bright red net. The net is known as mace — it is carefully separated from the nutmeg kernel and both are dried before being sold either whole or ground.

The liquid essence of nutmeg is obtained by steam distillation of the kernel. It has a distinctive odour, a sharp pungent taste and is made up of 80 per cent pinene and camphene, eight per cent terpenic alcohols (linalol, borneol, terpineol and geraniol) and four per cent myristicine including other substances such as safrol and eugenol.

The alkaloid myristicine can produce dangerous narcotic effects if too much nutmeg essence is taken.

A fixed oil known as nutmeg butter can be obtained by hot pressing the nutmeg kernels. It contains myristicine, butyrin, olein palmitine and stearine. An aromatic essence can also be extracted from mace and used in certain alcoholic drinks like mulled wine.

Both nutmeg and mace are used as

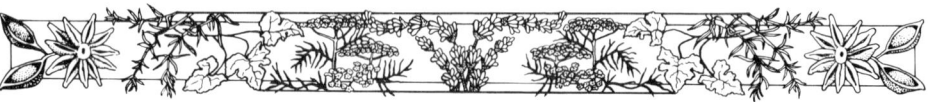

food flavourings, in potpourris and perfumes. Nutmeg is a carminative stimulant which can be helpful for colic, flatulence, vomiting, diarrhoea and other digestive difficulties. It particularly helps the absorption of starchy foods and fatty lamb. It has also been used to sweeten the breath. Externally it can be used to soothe the pain of rheumatism and arthritis and also for toothache.

Practical application

For digestive problems two drops of essence can be taken in honey after each meal. Alternatively nutmeg can be used in the meal itself as a flavouring. For rheumatic pains, nutmeg butter can be rubbed onto the painful area.

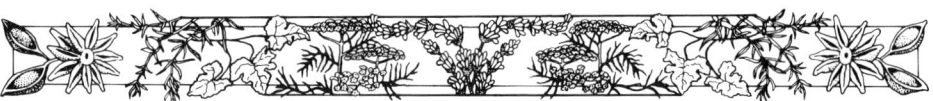

PENNYROYAL

Mentha pulegium

Pennyroyal is a species of mint indigenous to most parts of Europe. Its generic name is common to all mints, while its specific name *pulegium* comes from the Latin word *pulex* meaning flea, because it is highly effective in driving away fleas. Some scholars believe modern pennyroyal is the same plant as 'dictamne' which was known to the ancient Greeks and Romans. According to legend referred to by Virgil and other poets, deer wounded by huntsmens' arrows could be cured by eating this plant.

Pennyroyal has traditionally been popular with sailors. The dried leaves were used to freshen their drinking water and also to destroy the fleas which multiplied in their confined living quarters.

Until fairly recently pennyroyal was used to induce abortions. It was an important part of a witch's garland and to have it growing in the garden was said to give protection from the evil eye.

A low-growing plant, smaller than other mints, pennyroyal has small, shiny, rounded leaves and a strong peppermint scent. It is found growing in moist places, near streams and marshes, and forms a good ground cover in shady gardens. In spring it produces tall stems (about 30 cm high) which bear whorls of tiny purple flowers.

The essential oil, obtained by steam distillation, contains a significant amount of pulegone. It is similar to peppermint oil in taste and odour, except that it is more bitter, has a greenish-yellow colour and is slightly more toxic.

Pennyroyal is regarded by farmers as a dangerous plant as it is known to cause abortions if eaten by pregnant cattle. However, it is an excellent insect repellent and will keep away mosquitoes, ants and fleas.

The oil has a long history of use for female complaints. It is a uterine stimulant so should naturally be avoided by pregnant women although it is useful both during delivery and after childbirth to help expel the placenta. It is recommended for irregular or painful menstruation and for leucorrhoea. Its slightly analgesic qualities and its soothing effect on the nerves make it suitable for a number of complaints

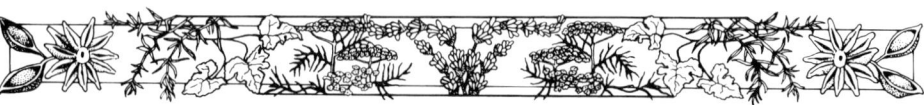

of nervous origin.

Pennyroyal helps digestive disorders, especially flatulence, colic and nausea. It is considered a liver and spleen tonic useful to promote the flow of bile and helps dissolve gall-stones. It is stimulating and warming and can be helpful for children with stomach or bowel upsets and to relieve mild fevers. Although it will promote sweating and reduce the temperature it is not as cooling as peppermint. It can be used to relieve spasms of coughing, especially whooping cough as it loosens mucus.

Used externally pennyroyal promotes local blood circulation and so helps to heal sores, boils, ulcers and also bruises. Diluted with water it will relieve itchiness, reddened skin and tinea. It soothes a toothache and has been recommended to ease the pain of aching thumbs.

Practical application

Pennyroyal is particularly effective as an insect repellent. The fresh leaves can be broken and rubbed on the skin or a few drops of the oil sprinkled on the sheets and bedding at night. Well diluted with water, the oil can be used to relieve the itchiness of insect bites and numb the pain of mouth ulcers.

PEPPERMINT

Mentha piperita

This is one of a number of different mints believed to have originally been a hybrid of watermint and spearmint. Its generic name is derived from the Latin word *mente* meaning 'thought', as it was believed to stimulate the brain. Mint is thought to have been introduced to Europe by the Arabs from North Africa and was an important medicinal and strewing herb for the ancient Egyptians, Greeks and Romans. The Greeks used it in their bath water and rubbed it into their dining-room tables before a meal, for as one Greek historian wrote, 'The smell of mint does stir up the mind and the taste to a greedy desire of meat.'

There is mention in the Bible of the Pharisees being paid tithes of mint, anise and cumin. After the plant was introduced to Britain by the Romans, references to it began to appear in English literature, including the works of Chaucer and Shakespeare. Records show that mint sauce, the traditional accompaniment to roast mutton, was used as early as the third century AD.

Different varieties of mint grow either wild or in gardens in most countries of the world. Peppermint has a typically mint-like appearance, with smooth pointed leaves tinged with purple and covered on the underside with fine hairs. It grows up to 60 cm tall, and has a strong characteristic smell and clusters of purple flowers which seldom bear seeds, so new plants must be propagated by breaking off runners.

Mint should be harvested just before coming into full flower. The essence is obtained by steam distillation of both the leaves and flowering tops. Its exact composition depends on the climate in which it has grown, with plants grown in cold climates generally producing stronger oils. The main constituents are: menthol (30–70 per cent), terpenes (menthene, phellandrene, limonene), a ketone (menthone) and tannin. One of the best quality oils is obtained from the Mitcham variety which is grown in England.

Peppermint oil is widely used both as a flavouring in confectionery and also in toothpastes and breath fresheners. As a healing agent, it is often suggested as a substitute for aspirin. It is antispasmodic, antiseptic and carminative and acts on the digestive system to soothe indigestion, flatulence, stomach pains and diarrhoea. A well-known remedy for travel sickness, it can also be helpful for nausea during pregnancy.

It stimulates the nervous system and can be taken as a general tonic as well as for shock and nervous debility. For centuries, mint tea has been an important drink in Arab countries, and its use is becoming much more widespread in the west. It is claimed by some to help build up a resistance to colds if taken regularly, but others find it disturbs their sleep if taken in large doses or for too long.

Peppermint can be used as an inhalant for asthma, bronchitis and sinusitis, and to help clear the stuffiness and headaches associated with colds as well as to mask bad breath. It can be used to soothe the patient and reduce fevers and is sometimes helpful for painful or scanty periods. In some Arab countries it is thought to increase virility and overcome impotence.

Used externally peppermint is excellent to relieve toothache as well as to soothe skin irritations and inflammations. It is an effective insect repellent.

Practical application

To make an effective inhalation for bronchitis and other respiratory complaints, add a teaspoon of mentholated alcohol to 100 ml hot water. (The menthol alcohol can be made by adding 60 ml essence of mint to 1000 ml of a solution of 80 per cent alcohol. It can be strengthened by adding 40 ml eucalyptus essence.)

If preferred, mint essence can be taken internally in doses of five drops on a little sugar between meals.

Many kinds of indigestion can be helped by a dose of three drops of mint essence after each meal.

For a simple and safe insect repellent, especially suitable for children and those anxious to avoid the potentially toxic effects of commercial insect sprays, simply sprinkle a few drops of peppermint essence on the pillow and sheets at night.

PINE (SCOTS PINE, NORWAY PINE)

Pinus sylvestris

This is the typical pine tree found in the cold mountainous areas of northern Europe, especially Scandinavia and the USSR. In Britain it is often incorrectly called the Scotch fir as it grows wild in the Highlands of Scotland and is an emblem of many Scottish clans. Its generic name comes from the Latin word for tree.

According to classical mythology, the fertility god Attis castrated himself under a pine tree when thwarted in love, and his spirit passed into the tree. The pine cone has been believed to be sacred to the goddess of love and a symbol of good luck, fecundity and the phallic principle as well as a charm to guard against witchcraft. Twin pine trees are a symbol of fidelity and passionate love. Mythological figures associated with the pine include Neptune, Bacchus, Osiris, Poseidon and Pan.

Although it is native to northern Europe, this large ornamental tree has been successfully grown in parks and gardens in other parts of the world. It has reddish bark, grey-green needle-like leaves and sharp pointed cones. The male flowers are orange-yellow while the female flowers are a pinkish green.

The best quality essence is extracted by steam distillation from the needles of trees grown in Scandinavia and Russia. It is a very pale yellow and has a pleasant balsam-like smell. The principal ingredients are: pinene, sylvestrene, phellandrene and cadinene as well as bornyl acetate, pumilone, carene and limonene. The resin from the tree produces a different oil known as turpentine.

Pine essence is a well-known antiseptic used in soaps, bath preparations and disinfectants. Used medicinally it is particularly beneficial for respiratory disorders — colds, flu, bronchitis and asthma — and to clear the nasal passages of sinus sufferers.

It is also beneficial for urinary infections such as cystitis and prostatitis and as a general revitalising tonic. Pine essence, especially when mixed with lemon or juniper, has been used for rheumatism, gall stones, stomach cramps, rickets and even impotence.

Practical application

An excellent inhalant for bronchitis can be made from 15 g pine needle oil mixed with 1000ml of a solution of 90 per cent alcohol. Add one teaspoon of this to a basin containing 100 ml of boiling water, then breathe in for several minutes, preferably with the head covered by a towel.

For increased effectiveness the chest should be rubbed with olive oil containing 5 per cent pine needle oil. If an internal dose is preferred, five or six drops of essential oil can be taken on brown sugar after each meal. This dose is also suitable for asthma, flu, colic and cystitis.

The pain of rheumatism can often be relieved by rubbing the afflicted areas with pine needle oil and alcohol or by applying a cream made from 1000 ml sweet almond oil, 250 g white wax, 750 g distilled water and 20g essential oil of pine. An alternative is to add two drops each of pine essence, juniper and lemon to two teaspoons of soya oil and then rub the mixture onto the affected areas.

ROSE

Rosa damascena Damask Rose
Rosa gallica Red Rose
Rosa centifolia Cabbage Rose

The rose, with its numerous varieties and hybrids, is one of the oldest flowers known to man. There is evidence that rosehips, with their extremely high Vitamin C content, formed a significant part of the diet of a neolithic Essex woman whose remains have been dated at approximately 2000 BC.

Some of the legends which surround the rose are as exotic as the flower itself, as are the explanations concerning its origins. For the Greeks, the rose was said to have sprung from the blood of Adonis, while for the Turks, it was the blood of Venus, the goddess of love. In Muslim legend, it was the blood of Mohammed which was transformed into this fragrant flower. When Confucius died in 479 BC he is said to have had 600 books on rose care in his library. In ancient Egypt large jars of dried petals were placed in the tombs of the pharoahs to perfume their journey to the after-life. Roman brides were fond of rose garlands, as was the infamous emperor Nero. At his extravagant feasts rose petals were showered from the ceilings in such profusion that some inebriated guests were actually suffocated by the rain of petals.

Rose oil is said to have been accidentally discovered in Persia at a royal wedding feast. The reception took place beside a canal filled with rose water for the occasion. In the heat of the day the oil began to separate and float to the top. When this was collected its properties were recognised and production of rose oil soon began.

Rose oil is extremely expensive to produce and for this reason rose water is much more widely used. The best and most expensive oil is the Bulgarian Rose Otto which is distilled from *Rosa damascena*, a variety which will grow only in a small mountainous district in Europe. Thirty roses are needed to make one drop of this orange-green oil, while to make 30 g (1 ounce) 60 000 roses would be needed. Today most rose oil is produced from the red rose *Rosa gallica* which is cultivated mainly in Morocco.

Rose oil is one of the most antiseptic and least toxic essences so it is suitable for use on children. It is good for improving poor blood circulation and for skin disorders, especially dry, sensitive or inflamed skin. Diluted as rose water, it is useful in treating tired and red eyes and conjunctivitis. It is effective for digestive problems, constipation, nausea and especially liver disorders. Research in the USSR has shown that rose oil stimulates the formation of bile and may be useful in treating cholecystitis and jaundice. Menstrual irregularities and leucorrhoea will often respond to rose oil. Some people believe that rose oil gained its reputation as an aphrodisiac because it increases the production of semen. It also acts on the nervous system to reduce nervous tension, insomnia and depression and has been recommended for stress-related conditions such as peptic ulcers and heart disease.

Practical application

The relatively inexpensive rose water, made from an infusion of petals, is generally preferred for home use. However, hard skin can be softened by regular application of a well-diluted solution of vinegar to which 0.5 per cent rose essence has been added.

For sore throats, an astringent gargle can be made from an infusion of 40 per cent dried and chopped petals. Rose honey (made by heating 100 g honey with an infusion made from 100 g petals in 100 g boiling water) can also be soothing.

ROSEMARY

Rosmarinus officinalis

Originally a Mediterranean plant widely used by the ancient Greeks and also by the Romans who introduced it to Britain. A plant full of symbolic significance, it has been associated with a rich folklore. As a traditional symbol of fidelity, friendship and remembrance, it was carried at old Anglo-Saxon weddings and funerals and is still worn on Anzac Day and Remembrance Day. Students in ancient Greece and Rome took a rather more literal interpretation of the powers of this herb and often wore a wreath of rosemary around their heads while studying for exams, to improve their memories. One of the less plausible stories used to illustrate the amazing restorative powers of rosemary comes from the year 1370. A seventy-year-old princess, suffering from gout and almost paralysed, is supposed to have taken the oil, known then as 'Water of the Queen of Hungary' whereupon she found herself transformed into a seductive maiden who became the bride of a Polish king.

Several legends surround the actual cultivation of the plant. It has been said that the bush will never grow taller than the height of Christ, that it will grow only in the garden of a righteous person and that it flourishes best in those gardens where 'the mistress is the master'. Some stories claim that rosemary was used to awaken the Sleeping Beauty. Sicilian peasants claimed that baby fairies lived in rosemary bushes and in some early Christian churches branches of rosemary were hung as a sign of welcome to any elves or fairies.

Although, as its Latin name suggests, rosemary grows particularly well near the sea, it can be cultivated in any mild, sunny climate. While it grows wild in many countries around the Mediterranean Sea, especially France, Spain and the Dalmatian Islands, the best quality oil is made from rosemary grown in Tunisia.

The plant has stiff, narrow dark green leaves, tiny pale blue flowers and a very strong aromatic scent. Its leaves are often used in cooking, especially to flavour lamb, and are also used in infusion both as a herbal medicine and as a cosmetic aid.

The essential oil is obtained by

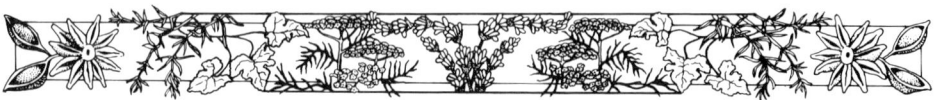

steam distillation of the flowering tops and leaves. About 100 kilograms of plant are needed to produce 1.5 kilograms of essence. This oil contains up to 15 per cent borneols, as well as camphene, camphors, cineol, lineol, pinene, resins, saponin and a bitter principle. Not all oil marketed as rosemary oil is of pure quality; some has been mixed with turpentine, sage and spike oils. The pure oil is also used in Eau de Cologne and other perfumes.

Rosemary oil has been used medicinally for hundreds of years. It is a general stimulant which can be used for a variety of nervous disorders, particularly tension headaches, palpitations, depression, general fatigue and short-term memory loss. It is helpful for disorders of the liver, gall stones, indigestion and stomach pains due to flatulence and its diuretic action helps reduce obesity due to fluid retention. Rosemary oil will sometimes bring on delayed periods. Its antispasmodic qualities make it helpful for respiratory complaints such as asthma, bronchitis, colds and flu. Externally it can be very soothing for rheumatism, arthritis and aching muscles. It can also be used to cleanse wounds and sores, to stimulate hair growth and to eradicate dandruff and other scalp disorders.

Rosemary oil is very potent and large doses can cause seizures and even death.

Practical application

For general debility and fatigue three or four drops of rosemary oil can be taken with honey or brown sugar before each meal. The effect of this treatment is enhanced if the back is also massaged with rosemary oil in alcoholic solution or with a special cream made from essence of rosemary and sweet almond oil combined with white wax and distilled water.

Rheumatic pains can often be eased by a hot compress which has been soaked in boiled water containing 2 per cent rosemary essence. An equally effective treatment is a soothing rub with a liniment made from 60 g spirit of rosemary, 2 g essence of origanum and 40 g tincture of ginger.

SAGE

Salvia officinalis

There are several different species of this well known herb whose healing and culinary uses have been known for centuries. Its generic name is derived from the Latin verb *salveo* — 'I save or heal' — and its power to do so has been highly regarded in different parts of the world. An ancient Arabic proverb asks 'How shall a man die who has sage in his garden?' while according to an old English rhyme 'He that would live for aye, must eat sage in May'. The ancient Egyptians and also the Chinese used it medicinally as a brain tonic and the Emperor Charlemagne thought so highly of its powers that he promoted its cultivation throughout his domains. Sage was also believed to soothe grief and its leaves were strewn around gravestones as a sign of remembrance.

Originally found on the northern shores of the Mediterranean, it is now grown in temperate climates all over the world. The highest quality sage is said to be that produced in the Dalmatian region of Yugoslavia where its cultivation is an important village industry. The plant itself is a hardy perennial shrub with long hairy greyish-green leaves and pale blue or lilac flowers.

The leaves are frequently made into a refreshing tonic tea and have also been widely used to clean the gums. Their essential oil contains up to 50 per cent thujone, tannin, an oestrogenic principle, borneol, salviol, cineol and salvene. This oil can be toxic and may induce epileptic fits so many therapists prefer to use the oil from clary sage, *Salvia sclarea*, which has similar properties but is not so potent.

Sage is a general tonic useful for irritability, tension headaches, nervous indigestion, loss of appetite and constipation. It is often used for menstrual difficulties and during childbirth to regulate labour and relax the mother. It is very effective in drying up the flow of breast milk and therefore should be avoided by mothers who are breastfeeding unless they have had to wean their baby suddenly. The antiseptic properties of sage make it useful for sore throats, inflamed skin, wounds and insect bites. For patients who are convalescing after a fever it can be used both to help them regain their strength and to reduce uncomfortable night sweats. Profuse sweating of the hands, feet and armpits can also sometimes be controlled by its use. Sage leaves burnt over charcoal can be used to disinfect a room after an infectious disease.

Practical application

An infusion of approximately 20 g of sage flowers and leaves, added to 1 litre of boiling water and left for ten minutes, can be taken as a general tonic, one cup three times a day. Sage is also available in a tincture; thirty to forty drops of this can be taken in a small amount of hot water twice a day. Two to four drops of sage essence in a teaspoon of honey can be taken three times a day. This dose is also suitable to dry up milk secretion. To treat wounds and ulcers, first wash with boiled water and 2 per cent sage essence, then cover with an ointment made from 25 g sage essence, 750 ml distilled water, 250 g white wax and 1000 ml olive oil.

TARRAGON

Artemisia dracunculus

Tarragon is known for its use as a culinary herb, particularly in French cooking. According to ancient legend this herb made its first appearance when the seed of a flax plant was put into a radish root and planted in the ground to germinate. Its name is derived from the French word 'estragon' meaning 'little dragon' because it was used to cure the bites and stings of snakes, mad dogs and venomous insects.

Originally grown in France, it was introduced to Britain in the sixteenth century and became a popular salad plant in Tudor England. The poet Margaret Brownlow wrote

'... For few

Can resist the charm

Of a sprig of balm

Or the hope of becoming a paragon

By the tactful use of tarragon.'

The Russian tarragon *Artemisia dracunculoides* which originated in Siberia and southern and western Asia is a larger plant, growing up to 1.5 metres tall, and being less fragrant, is used in greater quantities.

French tarragon has long narrow shiny leaves which grow on thin stalks and tend to form a tangled bush. The small yellowish flowerbuds rarely open into full bloom and the plant dies away to ground level in winter. The leaves should be harvested before they begin to turn yellow, and can be used fresh or dried in cooking.

The essential oil can be obtained by distillation of the plant. It contains up to 60 per cent estragole, 15–20 per cent terpenes as well as phellandrene, ocimene, methylchavicol and herniarin.

Tarragon oil is a general digestive stimulant, which helps promote a healthy appetite, prevents indigestion, flatulence and colic and sweetens the breath. It is an internal antiseptic and antispasmodic and can also be used to expel intestinal worms. Tarragon essence on a lump of sugar can be taken to cure hiccups. People on a salt-free diet are often advised to use tarragon. The herb has been said to possess anti-cancer properties though this has not been experimentally verified.

If fresh tarragon is available its beneficial qualities can most easily be obtained by eating it raw in salads

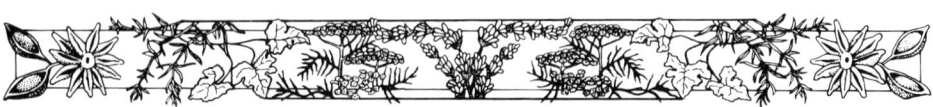

or soups. It can also be taken in an infusion of 25–30 g to a litre of water, but this is not very strong and it may be necessary to add a drop of essence to each cup.

Practical application

To stimulate a poor appetite, particularly during convalescence, four drops of essence can be taken on a little brown sugar half an hour before each meal. To expel intestinal worms five drops of essence can be taken three times a day between meals. A lukewarm enema of boiled water and olive oil with 10 per cent tarragon essence is also effective.

TEA-TREE OIL

Melaleuca alternifolia

In 1925, the New South Wales government scientist Arthur Penfold announced an important discovery. He had just completed a three-year period of laboratory testing and had found a species of tea-tree whose antiseptic properties were thirteen times stronger than carbolic acid — the main antibacterial weapon of the day. He also noted that only the trees growing in the Bungawalbyn wetlands valley near Coraki, in northern New South Wales, had the appropriate medicinal concentration.

Penfold's findings stimulated further medical research and led to the establishment of around thirty stills in and around the valley. The best tea-tree oil in the world still comes from this district — a relatively small area of 200 square kilometres.

The healing properties of tea-tree oil were known to the Bundjalung Aborigines and are far-ranging. Tea-tree oil can be used for a variety of complaints including sinus congestion, pimples, mouth ulcers, cold sores, tinea, stings, burns, sore throats, cuts and infections, sunburn and thrush.

The method for extracting the oil is quite simple. The leaves are harvested using a cane knife and this ensures that no damage is done to the plant itself; indeed, some trees have now been harvested for nearly sixty years. The leaves are then steamed in vats over slow burning log fires and the steam releases oil vapour from the glands in each leaf. The steam and vapour are channelled through a coil immersed in cold water, and in due course the water and liquid oil pass into a still. Here the oil floats to the surface where it can be skimmed off and filtered for purification. Ten litres of oil can be produced from a tonne of tea-tree leaves.

The original tea-tree cutters in the wetlands of Bungawalbyn Creek used the oil to ward off leeches and also to treat skin irritations on their feet, legs and arms. Later, dentists began to use the oil as a standard mouthwash and it was really only because of the discovery of penicillin and the rise of antibiotics that tea-tree oil was forgotten. Since 1976, however, a company called Thursday Plantation has been busy replanting selected trees, and redeveloping the

Bungawalbyn Creek region for the commercial distribution of tea-tree oil. The United States government has now approved the use of the oil in cosmetics and there is considerable scope in export markets. The oil can be used, for example, in shampoos, soaps, antiseptic creams, and even in anti-itch treatments for pets!

Practical application

For cuts, infections, burns, pimples, tinea and stings, the oil can be dabbed onto the affected area two to three times a day until the complaint clears. For sinus congestion the oil can be applied to the sinus area or inhaled using a vaporiser or steam bath.

For sore throats place five drops in quarter of a glass of juice, gargle and swallow slowly. Do this two to three times over a twelve-hour period. In the case of sunburn it is advisable to dilute the oil (five drops in 25 ml of water) and spread over the affected parts. A dilution is also appropriate for treating vaginal thrush. Make a 5 ml in 500 ml douche, shake vigorously, and apply to the vagina. Alternatively, add 5–10 ml to a sitz bath and flush in and around the vagina.

THYME

Thymus vulgaris, Thymus serpyllum

An aromatic perennial herb, thyme has been popular since ancient times, especially among the Greeks and Romans. The name itself is thought to derive from the Greek *thymon*, meaning 'fumigate', and the herb was used to make incense in the temples. Wild thyme grew on the hills near Athens and the Greeks revered the honey produced by the bees who drew nectar from these plants. Later the Romans took thyme to Britain, where it became popular as a culinary and medicinal herb. And in the seventeenth century it once again became popular through its association with bees; Gervas Markham recommended that hives could be perfumed with its scent. Wild thyme has also been used for aromatic lawns.

Common thyme, *Thymus vulgaris*, has pink and lilac flowers and is indigenous to the Mediterranean regions and southern Europe although it also grows in mild climates in many other countries. Wild thyme, *Thymus serpyllum*, resembles common thyme but has a slightly more lemon-like odour and is native not only to Europe but also to northern and central Asia. Both belong to the family *Labiatae* and the essential oil of both varieties can be used for the healing functions described here.

Thyme oil is extracted from the flowers of the plant through steam distillation and is strongly antiseptic. It contains carvacrol, thymol and pinene and has been widely used as a disinfectant and rubefacient for muscular problems, sprains and rheumatism. It has a strong cleansing and astringent action on the skin, tightening the surface and helping to remove blemishes like pimples and blackheads. Thyme oil is also suitable for treating infections like ringworm, eczema and psoriasis.

However, thyme oil also has other health functions. It is useful for treating whooping cough, colds and bronchial complaints and it is thought that the oil stimulates the production of white blood corpuscles, thus aiding resistance to infectious diseases. It also helps lower blood pressure and can be used to treat nervous complaints like insomnia and depression. A few drops massaged onto the forehead can provide temporary relief from headaches.

Practical application

For *internal* use to stimulate circulation, as an inhalant for nervous tension or as an expectorant for bronchial complaints, take three to five drops of essential oil, either in an alcoholic solution or in honey water.

For *external* use on boils, sores, sprains, as a skin disinfectant or for rheumatism, massage a few drops onto the affected area — but take care to avoid the eyes. Thyme can be used 50:50 with almond oil.

YLANG-YLANG

Cananga odorata

The beautiful yellow flower of this tree, with its exotic scent which is somewhat similar to a mixture of jasmine and almond blossom, has earned the name 'flower of flowers'. The trees on which they grow can be up to twenty metres tall and are found in Indonesia, the Philippines, Madagascar, Réunion and the Comoro Islands, with the finest oil being produced from the flowers of trees grown near Manila in the Philippines. The tree blossoms all year but the best flowers are those picked in May and June, early in the morning. Oil from Javanese trees is generally considered quite inferior.

Oil of ylang-ylang, obtained by steam distillation of the flowers, is a yellowish colour with a slightly bitter taste. Its main constituents are: linalol, safrol, eugenol, geraniol, pinene, sesquiterpenses, cadinene, benzoate of benzyl, and combined acetic, benzoic, formic, salicylic and valeric acids.

A pleasant-smelling oil whose odour is said to soothe anger and frustration, it is often used in perfumes and bath oils and is an ingredient in the famous Macassar hair oil. Ylang-ylang oil has a calming effect on the nervous system and is recommended for anxiety, tension, insomnia, high blood pressure and accelerated breathing (hyperpnoea) and heart rate (tachycardia). It is also considered an aphrodisiac and is believed to be helpful in overcoming impotence and frigidity. The oil has some antiseptic qualities and can be used for intestinal infections. It makes a pleasant-smelling oil for facial massage and is particularly good for oily skin. However, some people find the odour rather overpowering in large quantities and it can cause headaches and nausea.

Practical application

For hypertension, three drops of ylang-ylang essence can be taken with brown sugar or honey or in an alcoholic solution after every meal. A stronger dose — four to five drops — can be used to treat intestinal infections.

INCENSES

Incenses are made from fragrant essential oils and resins and are used to elevate the senses, both emotionally and spiritually. Among the most popular incenses are such flower-based oils as rose, lavender and ylang-ylang; resins like frankincense, vetiver, styrax and myrrh; leaf essences like geranium, rosemary and sage, and berry essences like coriander, cloves and caraway.

Incenses stimulate our olfactory awareness and have been used since earliest times in healing ceremonies, magical evocations and religious rites. As incenses are usually burned on charcoal and the smoke rises, like prayers, to the heavens, the fragrances released in this way were believed to please the gods and banish evil forces. At Heliopolis in ancient Egypt, different types of incense were burned to honour Ra : resin in the morning, myrrh at midday and sacred *kyphi*, or *kuphi*, at sunset. (*Kyphi* consisted of sixteen ingredients, including honey and wine, and was mixed by the priests according to a secret formula.)

In Muslim countries incense is sometimes burned at funerals, and is used to ward off the Evil Eye, while in India it is used as an accompaniment to meditation — the fragrances providing a pleasant ambience for the expansion of consciousness.

Incenses have also played a religious role in the West.

From the *Book of Exodus* (Chapter 30) we gain an insight into their use in Hebrew culture:

And the Lord said unto Moses: Take unto thee sweet spices, stacte and onycha and galbanum; these sweet spices with pure frankincense; of each shall there be like weight, and thou shalt make it a perfume, a confection after the art of the apothecary, tempered together, pure and holy; and thou shalt beat some of it very small. And as for the perfume which thou shalt make, ye shall not make to yourselves according to the composition thereof: it shall be unto thee holy for the Lord.

The Hebrews were indeed forbidden to use this special incense formula for personal use — it was strictly intended for a sacred ceremonial purpose.

The ancient Greeks and Romans were similarly fond of incense and

perfumes, and knowledge of these healing arts was said to have passed from the immortals to humankind via Aeone — one of Aphrodite's nymphs. The Emperor Nero's fondness for the fragrance of roses is legendary (see entry 'Rose' in *Herbal Oils*), and incenses were burned in honour of the household gods, or *lares*.

Incenses also play a part in some forms of Christian worship. Although perfumed candles date back to the fourth century, it was not until the fifth century that incense was introduced. By the fourteenth century incense featured in the High Mass and in services such as Vespers, and was also used to consecrate churches. Incense remains a distinctive feature of ritual in the Eastern Orthodox Church, in Roman Catholicism and in 'high church' Anglican ceremonies.

However, incense does not need to be used only in a ceremonial religious setting. It can be employed at home simply to provide a room with a special fragrance, to lift one's spirits, and to aid meditation.

Most people who enjoy the fragrance of incense agree that one should adopt a peaceful frame of mind and, according to one's personal preferences, say a prayer, mantra or 'affirmation' to accompany its use. Incenses linger in the air and may serve as a positive reminder that a particular room is used for one's 'quiet time' — for meditation or spiritual contemplation. Incense may also be used to provide a pleasant fragrance in rooms used for healing therapies like massage and rebirthing.

Method for burning incense

Take a charcoal block, light it on the corner or edge and place it in a metal incense burner. Do not hold the charcoal in your hand after lighting, because it contains a quick-lighting agent. When the whole tablet has 'caught', blow gently across it until it glows and then pour a few drops of fragrant oil onto the warm surface. Alternatively use a half teaspoon of incense granules. One block of charcoal usually suffices for a meditation and when the ingredients have burned down, place the burner and its contents outside your room.

The following incenses are especially popular:

Children: ginger, petitgrain, rose, spearmint, tea-tree

Concentration and willpower: cedarwood, ginger, sage

Devotional use: boronia, jasmine, neroli, rose, ylang-ylang

Feminine influence: bergamot, geranium, jasmine, rose, lavender, ylang-ylang

Festivities and weddings: boronia, jasmine, neroli, rose

General healing: juniper, lemon, mace, mandarin, rose, sandalwood, wintergreen

Masculine influence: cedarwood, ginger, juniper, pine

Mental healing: bergamot, cajeput, lavender, lemon, rose, sandalwood, ylang-ylang

Meal-times and dinner parties: ginger, lemon, lime, orange

Meditation: bergamot, jasmine, lavender, patchouli, rose, sandalwood, ylang-ylang

Mental stimulation: pine, rosemary

Moon-type meditations: jasmine, lavender, patchouli, ylang-ylang

Music: cloves, geranium, pine, spearmint

Psychic work: bergamot, lavender, lemongrass, petitgrain, sandalwood

Physical healing: cinnamon, mace, mandarin, pennyroyal, thyme

Relaxation: cajeput, lavender, lemongrass, pine

Sun-type meditations: cloves, orange, pine

Purification: cinnamon, lemon, lime, mace, sandalwood

FLOWER
ESSENCES

Bach Flower Remedies

Although the term 'flower essences' sounds somewhat similar to 'essential oils' they are not the same thing. Closer conceptually to homeopathic remedies, in which the activating agent is increasingly distilled, flower essences provide a type of 'vibrational healing' intended as a treatment for emotional imbalance. Basically, flower essences are extracts of flowers made in water and are used for mental and spiritual problems. Practitioners believe that the life-force of the flower is attracted into the water, and that this life-force also carries with it vibrational qualities useful for restoring health.

The pioneer of flower essences was Dr Edward Bach (1886–1936) and his healing remedies were based on English wildflowers. However, since his death there has been increasing interest in flower essences, and practitioners in the United States and Australia have also developed their own, indigenous remedies.

Dr Bach studied at Birmingham University and University College Hospital, London. Having graduated as a physician he set up a consulting practice near Harley Street but rapidly became disillusioned with orthodox medicine. He began to see that with his patients it was not the disease symptom that was the problem, but the negative mental condition underlying it. Dr Bach turned for a time to bacteriology and gained some eminence in the field, but still found that he was not penetrating deeply enough. Disease seemed to have a psychosomatic origin. He felt it was 'our fears, our cares, our anxieties and such like, that open the path to the invasion of illness'.

Then he learnt of the work of the German physician Samuel Hahnemann (1755–1843), the founder of homeopathy, who had said 'The patient is the most important factor in his healing'. Bach was impressed by Hahnemann's *The Organon of Medicine* and worked for a time at the Royal Homeopathic Hospital. He came increasingly to adopt the view that patients had to be treated not in terms of their physical ailments but their emotional condition. Bach, in looking for remedies to restore peace of mind to his patients, turned to Nature for his guidance. In his book *Heal Thyself* he wrote:

> Among the types of remedies that will be used will be those obtained from the most beautiful plants and herbs to be found in the pharmacy of Nature, such as have been divinely enriched with healing powers for the mind and body of man.

Bach visited Wales in 1928 and beside a mountain stream gathered such flowers as impatiens and mimulus, and also discovered wild clematis. He then made essences from these specimens which he later gave to his patients.

Encouraged by the initial success of his remedies, Dr Bach abandoned his practice in London in 1930 and decided instead to roam around the fields and meadows of the countryside looking for flowers which might have healing qualities. To his surprise, Bach found that as he held his hand over a flowering plant he began to feel that he was acquiring its properties and altering his mood. Sometimes the properties were positive, other times negative. Over a seven-year period Dr Bach isolated 38 flowers that appeared to have qualities that could benefit a range of emotional afflictions such as fear, loneliness, exhaustion, impatience, intolerance and restlessness.

Many of the flowers grew wild in the fields, blooming in bright sunlight. Bach would take the heads of the flowers and place them upon the surface of water contained in a glass bowl. Here they would remain for three hours, absorbing the sunlight and, so he believed, transferring some of their life-force into the water. Bach then removed the flowers and gathered the water for subsequent use. In the case of blossoms growing on trees another method applied. These flowers would be placed in a sterile saucepan, covered with water, and gently boiled for 30 minutes. They were then similarly removed and the water bottled, often with the addition of a small quantity of brandy acting as a preservative.

Dr Bach placed his remedies under seven headings, which for him identified major emotional and psychological states. He also referred to the first twelve plants he discovered as 'the twelve healers'.

Since the following text is the pioneering statement on flower essences we include here Dr Bach's own description of each remedy. This forms part of Bach's short work *The Twelve Healers*, and the twelve healers themselves are asterisked. Although not included in the original text, the botanical names of the plants are also given:

THE 38 REMEDIES

are placed under the following 7 headings

1 FOR FEAR
2 FOR UNCERTAINTY
3 FOR INSUFFICIENT INTEREST IN PRESENT CIRCUMSTANCES
4 FOR LONELINESS
5 FOR THOSE OVER-SENSITIVE TO INFLUENCES AND IDEAS
6 FOR DESPONDENCY OR DESPAIR
7 FOR OVER-CARE FOR WELFARE OF OTHERS

For those who have fear

*ROCK ROSE

(*Helianthemum nummularium*)

The rescue remedy. The remedy of emergency for cases where there even appears no hope. In accident or sudden illness, or when the patient is very frightened or terrified, or if the condition is serious enough to cause great fear to those around. If the patient is not conscious the lips may be moistened with the remedy. Other remedies in addition may also be required, as, for example, if there is unconsciousness, which is a deep, sleepy state, Clematis; if there is torture, Agrimony, and so on.

*MIMULUS

(*Mimulus guttatus*)

Fear of worldly things, illness, pain, accidents, poverty, of dark, of being alone, of misfortune. The fears of everyday life. These people quietly and secretly bear their dread, they do not freely speak of it to others.

*CHERRY PLUM

(*Prunus cerasifera*)

Fear of the mind being over-strained, of reason giving way, of doing fearful and dreaded things, not wished and known wrong, yet there comes the thought and impulse to do them.

ASPEN

(*Populus tremula*)

Vague unknown fears, for which there can be given no explanation, no reason.

Yet the patient may be terrified of something terrible going to happen, he knows not what.

These vague unexplainable fears may haunt by night or day.

Sufferers are often afraid to tell their trouble to others.

RED CHESTNUT

(*Aesculus carnea*)

For those who find it difficult not to be anxious for other people.

Often they have ceased to worry about themselves, but for those of whom they are fond they may suffer much, frequently anticipating that some unfortunate thing may happen to them.

83

For those who suffer uncertainty

*CERATO

(*Ceratostigma willmottianum*)

Those who have not sufficient confidence in themselves to make their own decisions.

They constantly seek advice from others, and are often misguided.

*SCLERANTHUS

(*Scleranthus annuus*)

Those who suffer much from being unable to decide between two things, first one seeming right then the other.

They are usually quiet people, and bear their difficulty alone, as they are not inclined to discuss it with others.

*GENTIAN

(*Gentianella amarella*)

Those who are easily discouraged. They may be progressing well in illness or in the affairs of their daily life, but any small delay or hindrance to progress causes doubt and soon disheartens them.

GORSE

(*Ulex europaeus*)

Very great hopelessness, they have given up belief that more can be done for them.

Under persuasion or to please others they may try different treatments, at the same time assuring those around that there is so little hope of relief.

HORNBEAM

(*Carpinus betulus*)

For those who feel that they have not sufficient strength, mentally or physically, to carry the burden of life placed upon them; the affairs of every day seem too much for them to accomplish, though they generally succeed in fulfilling their task.

For those who believe that some part, of mind or body, needs to be strengthened before they can easily fulfil their work.

WILD OAT

(*Bromus ramosus*)

Those who have ambitions to do something of prominence in life, who wish to have much experience, and to enjoy all that which is possible for them, to take life to the full.

Their difficulty is to determine what occupation to follow; as although their ambitions are strong, they have no calling which appeals to them above all others.

This may cause delay and dissatisfaction.

Not sufficient interest in present circumstances

*CLEMATIS

(*Clematis vitalba*)

Those who are dreamy, drowsy, not fully awake, no great interest in life. Quiet people, not really happy in their present circumstances, living more in the future than in the present; living in hopes of happier times, when their ideals may come true. In illness some make little or no effort to get well, and in certain cases may even look forward to death, in the hope of better times; or maybe, meeting again some beloved one whom they have lost.

HONEYSUCKLE

(*Lonicera caprifolium*)

Those who live much in the past, perhaps a time of great happiness, or memories of a lost friend, or ambitions which have not come true. They do not expect further happiness such as they have had.

WILD ROSE

(*Rosa canina*)

Those who without apparently sufficient reason become resigned to all that happens, and just glide through life, take it as it is, without any effort to improve things and find some joy. They have surrendered to the struggle of life without complaint.

OLIVE

(*Olea europea*)

Those who have suffered much mentally or physically and are so exhausted and weary that they feel they have no more strength to make any effort. Daily life is hard work for them, without pleasure.

WHITE CHESTNUT

(*Aesculus hippocastanum*)

For those who cannot prevent thoughts, ideas, arguments which they do not desire from entering their minds. Usually at such times when the interest of the moment is not strong enough to keep the mind full.

Thoughts which worry and will remain, or if for a time thrown out, will return. They seem to circle round and round and cause mental torture.

The presence of such unpleasant thoughts drives out peace and interferes with being able to think only of the work or pleasure of the day.

MUSTARD

(*Sinapis arvensis*)

Those who are liable to times of gloom, or even despair, as though a cold dark cloud overshadowed them and hid the light and the joy of life. It may not be possible to give any reason or explanation for such attacks.

Under these conditions it is almost impossible to appear happy or cheerful.

CHESTNUT BUD

(Aesculus hippocastanum)

For those who do not take full advantage of observation and experience, and who take a longer time than others to learn the lessons of daily life.

Whereas one experience would be enough for some, such people find it necessary to have more, sometimes several, before the lesson is learnt.

Therefore, to their regret, they find themselves having to make the same error on different occasions when once would have been enough, or observation of others could have spared them even that one fault.

Loneliness

*WATER VIOLET

(Hottonia palustris)

For those who in health or illness like to be alone. Very quiet people, who move about without noise, speak little, and then gently. Very independent, capable and self-reliant. Almost free of the opinions of others. They were aloof, leave people alone and go their own way. Often clever and talented. Their peace and calmness is a blessing to those around them.

*IMPATIENS

(Impatiens glandulifera)

Those who are quick in thought and action and who wish all things to be done without hesitation or delay. When ill they are anxious for a hasty recovery.

They find it very difficult to be patient with people who are slow, as they consider it wrong and a waste of time, and they will endeavour to make such people quicker in all ways.

They often prefer to work and think alone, so that they can do everything at their own speed.

HEATHER

(Calluna vulgaris)

Those who are always seeking the companionship of anyone who may be available, as they find it necessary to discuss their own affairs with others, no matter whom it may be. They are very unhappy if they have to be alone for any length of time.

Over-sensitive to influences and ideas

*AGRIMONY

(Agrimonia eupatoria)

The jovial, cheerful, humorous people who love peace and are distressed by argument or quarrel, to avoid which they will agree to give up much.

Though generally they have troubles and are tormented and restless and worried in mind or in body, they hide their cares behind their humour and jesting and are considered very good friends to know. They often take alcohol or drugs in excess, to stimulate themselves and help themselves bear their trials with cheerfulness.

*CENTAURY

(*Centaurium erythraea*)

Kind, quiet, gentle people who are over-anxious to serve others. They overtax their strength in their endeavours.

Their wish so grows upon them that they become more servants than willing helpers. Their good nature leads them to do more than their own share of work, and in so doing they may neglect their own particular mission in life.

WALNUT

(*Juglans regia*)

For those who have definite ideals and ambitions in life and are fulfilling them, but on rare occasions are tempted to be led away from their own ideas, aims and work by the enthusiasm, convictions or strong opinions of others.

The remedy gives constancy and protection from outside influences.

HOLLY

(*Ilex aquifolium*)

For those who are sometimes attacked by thoughts of such kind as jealousy, envy, revenge, suspicion.

For the different forms of vexation.

Within themselves they may suffer much, often when there is no real cause for their unhappiness.

For despondency or despair

LARCH

(*Larix decidua*)

For those who do not consider themselves as good or capable as those around them, who expect failure, who feel that they will never be a success, and so do not venture or make a strong enough attempt to succeed.

PINE

(*Pinus sylvestris*)

For those who blame themselves. Even when successful they think they could have done better, and are never content with their efforts or the results. They are hard-working and suffer much from the faults they attach to themselves.

Sometimes if there is any mistake it is due to another, but they will claim responsibility even for that.

87

ELM

(*Ulums procera*)

Those who are doing good work, are following the calling of their life and who hope to do something of importance, and this often for the benefit of humanity.

At times there may be periods of depression when they feel that the task they have undertaken is too difficult, and not within the power of a human being.

SWEET CHESTNUT

(*Castanea sativa*)

For those moments which happen to some people when the anguish is so great as to seem to be unbearable.

When the mind or body feels as if it had borne to the uttermost limit of its endurance, and that now it must give way.

When it seems there is nothing but destruction and annihilation left to face.

STAR OF BETHLEHEM

(*Ornithogalum umbellatum*)

For those in great distress under conditions which for a time produce great unhappiness.

The shock of serious news, the loss of someone dear, the fright following an accident, and such like.

For those who for a time refuse to be consoled, this remedy brings comfort.

WILLOW

(*Salix alba ssp. vitellina*)

For those who have suffered adversity or misfortune and find these difficult to accept, without complaint or resentment, as they judge life much by the success which it brings.

They feel that they have not deserved so great a trial, that it was unjust, and they become embittered.

They often take less interest and are less active in those things of life which they had previously enjoyed.

OAK

(*Quercus robur*)

For those who are struggling and fighting strongly to get well, or in connection with the affairs of their daily life. They will go on trying one thing after another, though their case may seem hopeless.

They will fight on. They are discontented with themselves if illness interferes with their duties or helping others.

They are brave people, fighting against great difficulties, without loss of hope or effort.

CRAB APPLE

(*Malus sylvestris*)

This is the remedy of cleansing.

For those who feel as if they had something not quite clean about themselves.

Often it is something of apparently little importance: in others there may be more serious disease which is almost disregarded compared to the one thing on which they concentrate.

In both types they are anxious to be free from the one particular thing which is greatest in their minds and which seems so essential to them that it should be cured.

They become despondent if treatment fails.

Being a cleanser, this remedy purifies wounds if the patient has reason to believe that some poison has entered which must be drawn out.

Over-care for welfare of others

•CHICORY

(*Cichorium intybus*)

Those who are very mindful of the needs of others; they tend to be over-full of care for children, relatives, friends, always finding something that should be put right. They are continually correcting what they consider wrong, and enjoy doing so. They desire that those for whom they care should be near them.

•VERVAIN

(*Verbena officinalis*)

Those with fixed principles and ideas, which they are confident are right, and which they very rarely change.

They have a great wish to convert all around them to their own views of life.

They are stong of will and have much courage when they are convinced of those things that they wish to teach.

In illness they struggle on long after many would have given up their duties.

VINE

(*Vitis vinifera*)

Very capable people, certain of their own ability, confident of success.

Being so assured, they think that it would be for the benefit of others if they could be persuaded to do things as they themselves do, or as they are certain is right. Even in illness they will direct their attendants.

They may be of great value in emergency.

BEECH

(*Fagus sylvatica*)

For those who feel the need to see more good and beauty in all that surrounds them. And, although much appears to be wrong, to have the ability to see the good growing within. So as to be able to be more tolerant, lenient and understanding of the different way each individual and all things are working to their own final perfection.

89

ROCK WATER

(Solarised spring water)

Those who are very strict in their way of living; they deny themselves many of the joys and pleasures of life because they consider it might interfere with their work.

They are hard masters to themselves. They wish to be well and strong and active, and will do anything which they believe will keep them so. They hope to be examples which will appeal to others who may then follow their ideas and be better as a result.

Dr Bach spent the last two years of his life at Sotwell in Oxfordshire, and after his death his work was continued by Victor Bullen and Nora Weeks. Then, after their deaths in 1978 and 1975 respectively, the administration of the Bach Centre passed to Nickie Murray and her brother John Ramsell, the present curators. Even today, the Bach flower remedies are prepared according to Bach's original method and come from the original wildflower locations. The term 'Bach flower remedies' is now trademarked, and the authentic remedies are available only from the Bach Centre in Sotwell.

How to use the Bach flower remedies

Having identified your personality characteristics and the type of emotional problem or stress situation you are facing, the first step is to select the appropriate remedy concentrate. It is safe to take two or three drops of concentrate under the tongue, although many people find it equally effective to dilute the remedies with spring water. For example, a few drops of concentrate may be placed in a small glass of water and sipped at intervals until there is a noticeable improvement. The pattern for the diluted remedy is: four drops under the tongue four times a day — upon rising, between breakfast and lunch, between lunch and dinner, and then finally before going to bed. The Bach Centre recommends that the remedies be kept tightly sealed in their bottles, away from direct sunlight or extreme temperatures.

There is also a formula known as Rescue Remedy, developed by Dr Bach in the early 1930s and employing five of the 38 flower remedies (cherry plum, clematis, impatiens, rock rose and star of Bethlehem). It is the only combination remedy and is reported to have a positive calming and stabilising effect in a broad range of stressful situations, for example after accidents, bereavement etc.

Flower essences in the United States

Understandably, there have been other approaches to flower essences

around the world and some notable developments in the United States and Australia. As Dr Bach wrote in *Ye Suffer From Yourselves*, 'The action of these remedies is to raise our vibrations and open our channels for the reception of our Spiritual Self', and the philosophy of contemporary New Age flower essence healers is very similar. Shelley Merritt-Summers of the Santa Fe Flower Connection in New Mexico puts it this way:

> When an essence is taken into the body, the life force and vibrational quality is also carried into the body. It then interacts with vibrational qualities within the body or psyche. These interactions can express themselves in a variety of ways, depending on the essence taken and the effect you are trying to achieve, such as pulling joy into the body, or pushing anger out of the body. (*Health Foods Business*, 1986:46)

The 230 flower essence mixtures available from the Santa Fe Flower connection are much broader in scope than the Bach remedies, however, encompassing such southwestern essences as Oregon Grape for decisiveness, Golden Banner for changing rigid attitudes, Mariposa Lily for unity and completeness in relationships, and Butterfly Weed for developing spiritual sensitivity.

Pioneering work has also been performed by herbalist Richard Katz and his colleague Patricia Kaminski. Katz founded the Flower Essence Society (FES) in 1979 and since 1980 he and Kaminski have run the Society from Nevada City, California, as a centre of information, education and research into flower essences. The two practitioners draw much of their inspiration from Dr Bach but as they write in their article 'Flower Essences — Nature's Healing Language':

> Bach did not reveal much about his process of developing the essences, nor did he indicate a methodology that others might follow in deciphering the language of the flowers. Responding to the needs of our time, the Flower Essence Society has dedicated itself to the task of developing a new scientific methodology for investigating the subtle realm of plants, and for understanding how flower essences work within the body and soul of the human being.

Like Shelley Merritt-Summers, Katz and Kaminski emphasise the spiritual aspect of the essences and consider them to be especially useful for internal self-development:

> Because flower essences work deeply with one's inner being, their use requires a different awareness than do conventional medicines or even many 'holistic' remedies. Flower essences are chosen to assist people with their 'next step' in life, to break through limitations and actualise undeveloped potential. An accurate assessment of the client is essential, so that essences can be chosen that address the inner

changes the soul life needs to make. Sometimes this can produce what is called an 'awareness crisis', in which an issue is temporarily intensified before it can be worked through.

Katz had begun preparing essences from Californian garden and wild flowers as early as 1978, and he later shared his research findings with a small group of friends, practitioners and clients. The remedies gradually became known as the 'California Flower Essences' and in 1980 he decided to release twenty-four of the essences to the public. An effective communications network also evolved through the Flower Essence Society.

Of the 24 flower essences, eleven were native wildflowers (California poppy, iris, madia, penstemon, star tulip, yarrow, blackberry, manzanita, sagebrush, scarlet monkeyflower and sticky monkeyflower); five were naturalised wildflowers (wild chamomile or mayweed, scotch broom, red clover, self-heal, and wild sweet pea) and eight were garden flowers (borage, fuchsia, pink yarrow, sunflower, dill, morning glory, nasturtium and shasta daisy).

The following is a summation of the twenty-four California flower essences in alphabetical order:

BLACKBERRY

(*Rubus ursinus*) white/pink

For overcoming inertia, converting thoughts into actions and harnessing the creative faculties of the mind.

BORAGE

(*Borago officinalis*) blue

For confidence in facing dangers and challenges, for courage and the power to overcome discouragement or grief.

CALIFORNIA POPPY

(*Eschscholzia californica*) gold

For developing balanced inner development and overcoming restless outer seeking. Recognition that true spiritual knowledge lies within the heart.

CHAMOMILE

(*Anthemis cotula*) white/yellow

For developing inner calm and objectivity and releasing emotional tension. Also for nervousness and insomnia.

DILL

(*Anethum graveolens*) yellow

To help assimilate and integrate the impressions of life, especially when one feels overwhelmed by the pace of events.

FUCHSIA

(*Fuchsia hybrida*) red/purple

To help develop awareness and overcome blocked emotions. Also for

emotional repression which is manifesting as tension or psychosomatic illness.

IRIS

(*Iris douglasiana*) blue/violet

For artistic and creative inspiration, and for overcoming personal feelings of frustration and limitation.

MADIA

(*Madia elegans*) yellow/red spots

To aid concentration and attention to detail. Also for those who become easily distracted or sidetracked in their thought processes.

MANZANITA

(*Arctostaphylos viscida*) white/pink

For appreciation of the physical body and the material world. For those who are ambivalent towards physical things.

MORNING GLORY

(*Ipomoea purpurea*) blue/purple

For vitality, alertness and to ease restlessness. Useful for erratic energy and to help break old habit patterns.

NASTURTIUM

(*Tropaeolum majus*) orange/red

For vitality and emotional life. Useful for those who over-intellectualise.

PENSTEMON

(*Penstemon davidsonii*) violet/blue

For perseverance in relationships and to develop inner strength through adversity. To help overcome self-doubt when faced with challenges.

PINK YARROW

(*Achillea millefolum*) pink/purple

For those who drain psychic or emotional energy from others. Also for overcoming emotional over-sensitivity.

RED CLOVER

(*Trifolium pratense*) pink/red

To develop centredness and balance in emotionally-charged group situations. An antidote to panic or hysteria.

SAGEBRUSH

(*Artemesia tridentata*) yellow

For letting go of what is excessive or not essential in one's life. For releasing illusory self-images or expectations.

SCARLET MONKEYFLOWER

(*Mimulus cardinalis*) red

For the courage to face powerful emotions and bring them into a state of balance.

SCOTCH BROOM

(*Cytisus scoparius*)yellow

To aid motivation, perseverance and to help overcome pessimism and despair.

SELF-HEAL

(*Prunella vulgaris*) violet

For self-acceptance, self-confidence and to develop trust in one's inner health-creating forces.

SHASTA DAISY

(*Chrysanthemum maximum*) white/yellow centre

To help bring together diverse ideas into a unified whole.

STAR TULIP

(*Calochortus tolmiei*) white/purple

For overcoming resistance to the inner side of the self, and the spiritual realm in general. To help develop sensitivity and receptivity.

STICKY MONKEYFLOWER

(*Mimulus aurantiacus*) orange

For awareness of sexual issues, to overcome the fear of intimacy, and to help integrate sexual and loving feelings.

SUNFLOWER

(*Helianthus annuus*) yellow

To develop individuality while overcoming egotism or unbalanced self-effacement. Also useful for balancing one's relationship to father figures, and for the masculine principle in soul development.

SWEET PEA

(*Lathyrus latifolus*) red/purple

For overcoming social alienation or conflict, and to develop social responsiveness and belonging.

YARROW

(*Achillea millefolium*) white

For strengthening one's inner light in relation to feelings of disharmony or negativity. Also for those who feel vulnerable.

Katz does not maintain that his first 24 essences are an all-inclusive system nor that they replace the 38 Bach essences.

Rather, it is an expansion of the existing repertory of flower essences, in response to the needs of the times, which enables practitioners to make a more precise selection of the most effective essences for an individual at any particular time. It is a step in the development of a more universal understanding of flower essences and an invitation for other practitioners and researchers of sufficient attunement to participate in this process of discovery. (*The Flower Essence Journal*, Issue 4:69)

Since 1981 the FES has also begun to evaluate other flower essence remedies. Among them are such plant varieties as black-eyed susan, California pitcher plant, California wild rose, goldenrod, Indian paintbrush, quaking grass, saguaro, yerba santa and zinnia. Detailed summaries of plant essences are published periodically in *The Flower Essence Journal*.

Flower essences in Australia

In Australia, as in the United States, research into flower essences has a distinctly New Age flavour to it, and is often accompanied by other holistic healing therapies. For example, Western Australian flower essence therapist Vaasudeva Barnao also employs colour-healing in his practice; Sydney-based Ian and Kristin White use 'psychic channelling' techniques and are often drawn intuitively to the most appropriate wildflowers; and Queenslander, Roy Victor Love, acknowledges the inspiration of a 'divine force' while preparing his flower tonics.

Nevertheless, all of these practitioners relate very definitely to the pioneering work of Dr Bach, and believe that they are supplementing his findings with new remedies that relate specifically to the local environment.

Vaasudeva Barnao believes that there are many states of mind not covered by the Bach flower remedies and that Australian wildflowers can often fill this gap. He also avoids actually picking the flowers, preferring to utilise what he calls 'the vibration of live flowers'. In a recent interview with Cheryl Lange (*Nature & Health* Vol. 7 No. 1) Barnao explained that many plants appear to suffer distress when picked: 'It is my experience that this vibration also goes into the remedy when one uses picked flowers.' However, in other respects Barnao's method resembles Dr Bach's. In the same way as Bach, Barnao brings the flower into contact with the water in the presence of bright sunshine, and he similarly prepares a 'mother stock' from which further potions can be made.

Barnao found himself drawn towards colour-healing because he realised the significance of the form and colour of the plants. He also connects the symbolic colours with acupressure points and psychic force centres (*chakras*) in the body.

So far Vaasudeva Barnao has isolated around 60 flower essences which he uses in his practice. These include silver princess gum (for apathy); golden glory grevillea (for those who feel self-conscious); veronica (for deep loneliness); happy wanderer (for emotional or physical self-fulfilment); menzies banksia (for past pain intruding on one's life); geraldton wax (for developing mental independence), correa (for inner dissatisfaction), formosa orange (to help one experience 'the softness of life') and pincushion hakea (for those with fixed attitudes).

Roy Victor Love first heard about the Bach flower remedies in the 1950s from a family friend, Dr J.R. Atcherley. Atcherley was communicating regularly with Nora Weeks at the Bach Centre in England, and after Dr Atcherley died, Love's mother took over the distribution of Bach flower remedies. At that time there was only a modest demand for the remedies in Queensland, but Roy Love became increasingly interested in Bach's writings, and used the remedies himself for several years. Love now believes that, via the taste and smell receptors, the flower remedies help to fine-tune the emotional area of the brain, bringing about a harmony of mind and soul.

In 1961 Love had an unusual experience while wandering in the bush. He was many miles from his home at the time and was suddenly overwhelmed by an onslaught of mosquitoes. He panicked at first, but then felt that there must be an antidote somewhere near by. For ten minutes he searched fleetingly around, and then discovered a Moreton Bay cypress in full flower. As Love relates in his book *Folk Flower Tonics*:

The flowers of this tree looked very soothing to my troubled state of mind, and by placing a few flowers in my mouth I was just able to tolerate the annoyance of the mosquitoes. Soon after that, I prepared some of these flowers by boiling them for 20 minutes or so. I had no idea at the time that this would be the beginning of the 'Folk Flower Tonics' ... (Love, 1986:7)

Love actually developed his range of remedies many years later, in the early 1980s, and like Dr Bach prepares most of his tinctures using the sun-method. Three species, however, require boiling: the banksia, Moreton Bay cypress and crepe myrtle.

Love's range of flower-tonics include the following:

AGERATUM

(*Ageratum houstonianum*)

For loneliness, isolation and introversion.

BANKSIA

(*Banksia integrifolia*)

For adults or young children who have suffered trauma or illness and feel insecure as a result.

BROWN KNAPWEED

(*Centaurea jacea*)

For lack of confidence and indecision. Also for those who are too readily affected by other people's attitudes.

CREEPING LANTANA

(*Lantana montevidensis*)

For developing feelings of love and easing personal conflicts, especially among children.

CREPE MYRTLE

(*Lagerstroemia indica*)

For feelings of intolerance and for those disillusioned by the attitudes of others.

DAY LILY

(*Hemorocallis aurantiaca*)

For those facing seemingly insurmountable problems which need to be brought into manageable perspective.

IVORY CURL FLOWER

(*Buckinghamia celsissima*)

For irrational fears which one cannot easily pinpoint. These fears stem from an unknown cause.

MORETON BAY CYPRESS

(*Callitris columellaris*)

For feelings of panic, uneasiness or restlessness. Also useful for insect bites and for children who are teething.

PERSICARIA

(*Polygonum lapathifolium*)

To strengthen the mind during times of stress, and to help develop positive impulses and resolutions.

QUEEN OF THE NIGHT CACTUS

(*Epiphyllum strictum*)

To aid those who are suffering from guilt as a result of their spiritual beliefs. Also for those whose health 'hangs on a fine thread' following a crisis.

SENSITIVE PLANT

(*Mimosa pudica*)

To help overcome shyness, loneliness or introversion.

TANSY

(*Tanacetum vulgare*)

To help ease deep depression and doubts which are isolating oneself from a positive relationship with others.

WILD CARROT

(*Daucus carota*)

For those who feel 'the odd person out' in groups, and do not communicate easily with their peers.

Interesting research has also been carried out by Sydney naturopath Ian White and his wife Kristin — both of whom have used intuitive methods for discovering and classifying their 'Australian bush essences'.

Ian White comes from a family steeped in natural medicine. His great-grandmother and grandmother were both herbalists and his father was a chemist who specialised in herbal remedies. Ian himself has studied herbalism, iridology and homeopathy and is fascinated by 'psychic channelling' — opening the inner self to an influx of spiritual energy. With his wife Kristin, who is an artist and touch-for-health practitioner, he has explored different ways of tapping into the consciousness of plants and studying their intriguing healing properties.

About two years ago, Ian and Kristin were exploring the bushland in Frenchs Forest, north of Sydney. Ian was actually looking for waratahs but he and Kristin were powerfully drawn to the beautiful bush irises which presented a wonderful array of mauve and purple blooms. Mauve and purple belong on the spiritual end of the vibrational spectrum and Kristin says that she felt the bush iris seemed to provide a 'psychic doorway' to the other plant species — a type of entry to another level of awareness.

That particular afternoon there was time to prepare bush iris essence using Dr Bach's natural sunlight method, and this became the first of Ian and Kristin's 'Australian bush essences'. There are now 22 essences in their range, each of which is available in dosage or stock bottles. The Whites also distribute the traditional Bach flower remedies but they believe the bush essences have a special role to play in natural health and are especially relevant because the flowers grow in the local habitat.

There are minor differences between these essences and the Bach flowers, however. The Australian wildflowers require less sunlight-time when soaking in water, but Ian finds that a dosage of seven drops, three or four times a day, is required — whereas the Bach system uses only four drops. But the advantage is that the plants are close at hand. As Ian wrote recently in a magazine article, '. . . there is immense healing power in the Australian bush.' (*Wellbeing*, February, 1987)

These are the main qualities of the 'Australian bush essences':

DOG ROSE

(*Bauera rubioides*)

For those who feel shy or apprehensive and need to restore their confidence and love of life. Also for treating fear.

PAW PAW

(*Carica papaya*)

Useful if one feels unable to resolve problems. Stimulates assimilation and integration of new ideas.

FIVE CORNERS

(*Styphelia laeta*)

For low self-esteem. Helps to increase love and acceptance of oneself and promotes a sense of joyousness.

FRINGED VIOLET

(*Thysanotus tuberosus*)

For those recuperating. Also for those who resist physical contact after rape or assault. Reintegrates physical and psychic aspects of the self after trauma or shock.

SUN DEW

(*Drosera spathulata*)

For vagueness and disconnectedness. Ideal for stimulating attention to detail in those who are easily distracted or indecisive.

BOTTLE BRUSH

(*Callistemon linearis*)

For adolescents, parents and especially pregnant women who feel inadequate in major transitional points of life. Helps to develop positive feelings about pregnancy and to bond mother and baby during that phase.

WEDDING BUSH

(*Ricinocarpus pinifolus*)

For those who have difficulty in making commitments in relationships. Helps couples to come together in union, and strengthens life-purpose.

(NO COMMON NAME)

(*Philotheca salsofolia*)

For those who do not accept love or acknowledgement from friends or relatives. Helps one to 'open up' and allow oneself to have what one deserves.

BLACK-EYED SUSAN

(*Tetratheca ericifolia*)

For those with scattered energy — who are impatient and always rushing about their affairs. Promotes the ability to turn inward and become calm.

DRUMSTICK

(*Isopogon anethifolius*)

For those suffering from poor memory or who are unable to adapt past experiences to the present. Helps retrieve forgotten skills. Also useful for those with dominating personalities.

GREY SPIDER FLOWER

(*Grevillea buxifolia*)

For those experiencing terror and also those who fear the supernatural. Promotes faith, calmness and courage.

LITTLE FLANNEL FLOWER

(*Actinotus minor*)

For children who grow up too quickly, taking on the worries of the world, or for adults who deny the child in themselves. Allows children to be carefree and enjoy life, and encourages lightness and playfulness in adults.

SLENDER RICE FLOWER

(*Pimelea linifolia*)

For those prone to jealousy, racism or narrow-mindedness. Promotes humility, group harmony and the ability to see an overall plan in the beauty of life and individuals.

MOUNTAIN DEVIL

(*Lambertia formosa*)

For hatred, anger and those who hold grudges or are suspicious of others. Promotes unconditional love, acceptance and forgiveness.

WARATAH

(*Telopea speciosissima*)

For those who are in a state of deep despair — 'the dark night of the soul'. Promotes courage, faith and survival skills, enhancing one's ability to deal with personal disaster and chaos.

BUSH IRIS

(*Patersonia longifolia*)

For those who are unduly materialistic and are locked into the physical. Helps open channels to higher spiritual perceptions. Also useful for overcoming avarice, sexual excess or fear of death.

FLANNEL FLOWER

(*Actinotus helianthi*)

For those who feel physically uncomfortable being touched or in a crowd. It is especially useful for men who need to develop their own sensitivity in touching, and allows them to become more open and expressive with their feelings.

BLACKBOY

(*Xanthorrhoea arborea*)

Helps develop mental telepathy and access to mythic realms of consciousness, including the Aboriginal Dreamtime. Should be used with caution.

RED GREVILLEA

(*Grevillea speciosa*)

For those sensitive to criticism or who are overdependent on others. Promotes boldness and independence. Also for those 'stuck' in work situations or personal relationships.

BUSH FUCHSIA

(*Epacris longifolia*)

For those with complaints like dyslexia, stuttering or extreme nervousness. Helps develop clarity of thought, the ability to speak out, and quality of intuition. Balances left and right hemispheres of the brain.

(NO COMMON NAME)

(*Hibbertia pedunculata*)

For those who are inclined to use their knowledge to prove their superiority over others. Promotes more easy acceptance of one's own levels of understanding.

COMMON WISTARIA

(*Wistaria sinensis*) non-native

For males: useful for developing awareness of the feminine aspects of oneself.
For women: helpful for those who are sexually repressed and who need to relax and enjoy their sexual relationships.

Ian White believes that the best flowers to pick are those in full bloom and far removed from what he calls 'the polluting effects of civilisation' — roads, power lines, car fumes and chemicals. He also feels it is important to attune yourself to the plant and seek its permission to pick its flowers for a healing purpose.

Having gathered the flower essence Ian decants it into quality brandy to produce the 'mother tincture'. He then dilutes it in the same way as the Bach flower therapists. He says he has validated the bush essences over the last few years in spiritual healing groups where the treatments are tested intuitively, and also by using the muscle-test familiar to practitioners of applied kinesiology. Here the person either holds a bottle of essence in the hand or places a drop of essence on the tongue, and at the same time holds an arm forward, horizontal to the ground. A partner presses down on the arm as one resists. Authentic remedies test 'strong': the interior deltoid muscle locks in a positive way, indicating that the remedy is appropriate. Inappropriate remedies test 'weak', making it impossible to resist the downward pressure applied by the other person.

While not yet accepted in mainstream medicine, the bush essences and their Bach flower counterparts represent a significant spiritual and mental approach to healing, and have an increasing number of adherents — especially among naturopaths and practitioners of holistic health. The flower essences are on the opposite end of the spectrum from conventional medicinal drug treatments, depending not on a chemical effect so much as a vibrational response from the patient. Indeed,

101

for most flower essence devotees the treatments are much more than a medicine: they can contribute to the evolution of human consciousness.

Further information on flower essences may be obtained from the following sources:

In the United Kingdom

Dr Edward Bach Centre
Mount Vernon
Sotwell, Wallingford
Oxon OX 10 0PZ
England
ph (0491) 39 489

In the United States of America

The Dr Edward Bach Healing Society
461–463 Rockaway Avenue
Valley Stream, NY 11580
ph (516) 825 2229

Richard Katz and Patricia Kaminski,
Flower Essence Society,
PO Box 459,
Nevada City, CA 95959
ph (916) 265 9163

Shelley Merritt-Summers and Greer Glass
Santa Fe, Flower Connection Inc.
914 Baca, Suite B
Santa Fe, New Mexico 87501
ph (505) 984 1171

In Australia

Ian White
2/38 Benelong Road
Cremorne, NSW 2090
ph (02) 637 1628

Roy Victor Love
c/- Love Publications
43 Didcot Street
Kuraby, Queensland 4112
ph (07) 341 3592

Vaasudeva Barnao
Living Essences
PO Box 244,
Subiaco, WA 6008
ph (09) 381 9667

Essential Energies
16 Glebe Point Road
Glebe, NSW 2037
ph (02) 660 7008

FOOD OILS

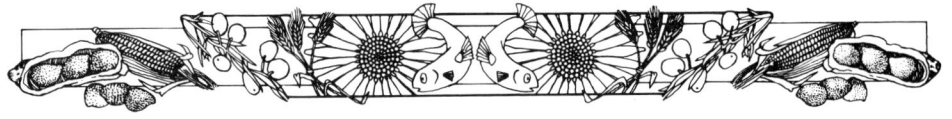

INTRODUCTION

Most of us appreciate that we should all reduce our intake of fat. However, since all oils are fats, doesn't that mean that the notion of 'healthy food oils' is a contradiction? The short answer is no.

As mentioned in the preface, there are good oils and bad oils, good fats and bad fats, and the important thing is to know how to distinguish them.

All common fatty acids are chemically similar to the extent that they contain between sixteen and eighteen carbon atoms in a chain. All of the carbon atoms between the first and the last are capable of having two hydrogen atoms attached, and from this various combinations become possible:

Saturated fatty acids have no double bonds. Here each carbon atom is linked to hydrogen atoms by single bonds.

Mono-unsaturated fatty acids have one double bond in their molecular structure. Oleic acid, for example, has a double carbon bond and on either side of this double bond a hydrogen atom is 'missing'.

Polyunsaturated fatty acids have more than one double bond in their structure. Linoleic acid, for example, has two double bonds, and arachidonic acid, four.

Saturated fatty acids are solid at room temperature and generally derive from an animal source. Examples of foods high in saturated fatty acids include butter, cream, hard cheese, dripping and lard.

Unsaturated fatty acids, on the other hand, are liquid at room temperature. The mono-unsaturated fatty acid, oleic acid, is found abundantly in olive oil, while polyunsaturated fatty acids are found in a number of vegetable oils, including safflower seed, sunflower seed, sesame, soybean, wheatgerm and corn. Indeed, polyunsaturated fatty acids are characteristic of vegetable oils, with the notable exceptions of palm and coconut oils, which are high in saturated fat. Polyunsaturated fatty acids also occur in various fish oils which, as we shall see, makes them especially relevant as a dietary means of combating coronary heart disease.

Which fats are most appropriate for human consumption? In 1983

the British National Advisory Committee on Nutritional Education (NACNE) published what are widely considered to be among the best researched dietary guidelines issued so far, and among the findings was a strong recommendation that we reduce our intake of saturated fats (C. Walker & G. Cannon, 1984). At present, the average intake of total fats accounts for around 38 per cent of total calories; according to NACNE that figure should not be more than 30 per cent. It also recommended that intake of saturated fats be limited to a maximum of 10 per cent of dietary energy. This means that we don't have to eliminate saturated fats altogether but simply keep them in perspective. On the other hand there are good reasons for utilising food oils high in polyunsaturated fatty acids — the oils which feature in the following pages of this book.

Why are polyunsaturated fatty acids important?

First of all, let's start with a definition. Foods can legally be labelled 'polyunsaturated' if polyunsaturated fatty acids exceed saturated by a ratio of 2:1. Obviously, since margarine is solid at room temperature, it contains constituents other than polyunsaturated fatty acids. In practice, 'polyunsaturated' products contain 40 per cent polyunsaturated fatty acids and less than 20 per cent fatty acids. Safflower seed oil has a particularly fine ratio of 7:1.

Polyunsaturated fatty acids help to reduce concentrations of cholesterol in the bloodstream. They are also essential for building membranes in the cells of the body and are precursors of prostaglandins — hormone-like substances which play a vital role in body chemistry.

The main examples of polyunsaturated fatty acids are linoleic, linolenic and arachidonic acids, which are known collectively as the 'essential fatty acids' because they are essential for life. None of these is produced by the body itself, although linolenic and arachidonic acids may be synthesised from other nutrients. Linoleic acid, however, must be obtained straight from the diet, and our focus in this chapter is on food oils which are rich in this particular fatty acid. Safflower seed oil, for example, is an especially rich source (75 per cent), as are soybean oil (52 per cent) and corn oil (56–59 per cent).

We all need around 5 grams of essential fatty acids in our diet each day, and if we don't have this intake the result may be rough or dry skin, dull hair, or abnormal nails. Polyunsaturated fatty acids are also important because of the role they play in reducing fatty deposits within the body. This is turn leads us directly to a consideration of dietary cholesterol and its links with atherosclerosis and coronary heart disease.

Dietary cholesterol

The fat we call 'cholesterol' is generally considered a 'baddie' in nutritional terms, but that is simplifying matters somewhat. As usual, it is a case of maintaining the right balance.

Cholesterol is produced in the body itself, helps to determine the properties of cell membranes, and also plays a part in the formation of steroid hormones, bile acids and Vitamin D. It is also a fact that between 50 and 80 per cent of dietary cholesterol can pass through the intestine without being absorbed, so it is necessary to understand how fats (lipids) are transported in the body and the role cholesterol plays.

Fats are insoluble in water, and in order to be transported by the blood they have to be modified. They associate with proteins (which *are* usually soluble in water) to form lipoproteins, and these in turn fall into two categories:

— Low density lipoproteins (LDL), which are the main carriers of cholesterol in the blood and transport cholesterol to the tissues.

— High density lipoproteins (HDL), which transport cholesterol away from the tissues to the liver, where it can then be excreted in bile.

This means that it is really our proportion of LDL cholesterol that we should be worried about, since it is these fatty deposits which will settle inside the walls of the arteries. As the arteries become increasingly clogged there is less room for the blood to flow through, and this condition is called atherosclerosis. If the clogging reaches a stage where blood clots are forming and the transport of blood to the heart is blocked altogether, the heart itself stops functioning and dies — the result is a 'heart attack'.

The importance of the healthy oils included in this chapter is that, with the exception of olive oil (which is included for other reasons), they are high in polyunsaturated fatty acids, which help to reduce the risk of atherosclerosis. Saturated fats in the diet, on the other hand, are more likely to cause the formation of blood clots which in due course can precipitate a heart attack.

The essential fatty acids mentioned earlier have the vital function of helping to reduce the adhesiveness of fatty deposits on the lining of the arterial wall. The prostaglandins which arise from the essential fatty acids also help to control the clustering of platelets in the blood. The latter produce the clotting effect which is important if we cut ourselves; without the action of platelets we would bleed to death. But on the other hand, we also need to guard against internal blood clots, since these could be equally deleterious.

Intake of dietary cholesterol is only one factor affecting blood cholesterol levels, and there are intrinsic mechanisms in the body which affect absorption, metabolism and excretion. For example, a vegetarian who began to eat egg yolks each day would notice an initial rise in blood cholesterol in the short term, but after eight weeks or so the level would return to normal. The body adjusts the amount of cholesterol produced in the liver to accommodate dietary intake. But like all things, it is wise not to stress the system, and there is no point in clogging up our body systems with large amounts of grease.

One of the things we *can* do is reduce our intake of saturated fats, and if we are utilising food oils, it is wise to choose those high in nutrients and polyunsaturated fatty acids. Most of these oils may be used in cooking, but only for short cooking times and only at low heats. Most require refrigeration if they are to be stored for extended periods although, fortunately, the Vitamin E present in most vegetable oils serves as a natural antioxidant.

How vegetable oils are extracted

As we have already noted, the main sources of polyunsaturated fatty acids are grains, beans and seeds. Several steps are involved in extracting the vital nutritious oil. First the raw seed comes to the refinery, where it is cleared and then shelled or hulled. The seeds are then cooked to break down the plant tissue; this makes the oil more accessible.

There are two basic methods of extraction:

The first of these methods (sometimes misleadingly referred to as 'cold-pressed') involves pressure by an expeller press. In this technique a heavy steel barrel presses the seeds against a surface which retains the pulp, while allowing the oil to sift through. Up to fifteen tons per square inch of pressure is applied and this results in heats between 65–150°C. When lower pressure techniques are employed, less oil is extracted so manufacturers favour the high pressure/high temperature method. Fortunately, even at a high temperature the oil retains most of its flavour and nutritional value.

The second method of extraction involves chemical solvents, the most common of which is a petroleum derivative named hexane. Hexane is volatile and toxic, but is used to flow through the toasted and flaked seed meal in order to dissolve and extract over 99 per cent of the oil present. During the process the oil solvent reaches a temperature of 60 °C; in order to evaporate the solvent the temperature is then raised to between 120–150 °C. This method is highly efficient but is unsuitable for oils with pleasant natural flavours because the removal of the solvent also kills the flavour of the oil! A variation on the method, known as the prepress-solvent method, allows the flavour to be preserved and it is this method which is favoured by commercial oil producers.

It is important to note that any vegetable oil which needs to be solid at room temperature has been hydrogenated. This involves treating the oil with hydrogen gas which changes the molecular structure and leads to more saturated fatty acid content. It is this process, for example, which keeps margarine hard, but it is the very hardness of it which reminds us that the food is not purely polyunsaturated, despite what the advertisements imply.

So what *are* the healthy food oils, and what do they contain? The following are profiles of the main oils which are of enduring benefit to our health — and they are worth noting because they rank among Nature's finest medicines!

CORN OIL

Corn, or maize (known botanically as *Zea mays*), was first cultivated in the West. It is the only native American grain and was known to the Aztecs, Incas and Mayans. Christopher Columbus was so impressed by it that he brought it with him back to Europe, and Europeans in turn were responsible for spreading it to Africa, Asia and the East Indies.

Each kernel of corn consists of a hard endosperm layer and a softer starchy interior. Corn is, however, surprisingly nutritious and includes such constituents as Vitamins A, B_1, B_2, C and E. The germ of the corn kernel has substantially more Vitamin E, iron, zinc and fibre than wheatgerm and it is also a good source of potassium, magnesium and copper. Corn is thought to be a good food for promoting the growth of bones, and the leaves of corn can also be wrapped around sores and wounds to draw out poisons and facilitate speedy healing.

Corn oil is usually extracted from the corn germ by means of steaming and pressing. However, some forms of corn oil also derive from the whole kernel and thus contain dark red gluten oil which comes from the hull. The resultant oil is orange, while pure corn germ oil is light yellow in colour.

Corn oil is approximately 85 per cent unsaturated and the fact that it contains 56–59 per cent linoleic acid and 1.6 per cent alpha-linolenic acid means that it helps to assimilate fat when used in cooking. It does tend to foam a little when heated but is ideal for baking, sautéing, and also in salads. Corn oil is in fact one of the most popular cooking oils and is produced commercially by the industries which use corn to produce glucose, corn starch and cereals.

Fortunately corn oil stores well as its high Vitamin E content helps to prevent oxidation.

FISH OIL

Omega-3 and EPA

A dietary paradox involving the Greenland Eskimos is responsible for what seems to be a major breathrough against heart-disease. The question first asked by Swedish scientists over a decade ago was: why should Eskimos who have a fat intake sometimes exceeding 600 grams per day, and a very high intake of flesh protein, not be prone to heart disease? The answer appears to be that Omega-3 fish oil, and in particular an important constituent called eicosapentaenoic acid (EPA), is a protecting factor.

Most of the fat in the Greenland Eskimo diet is obtained from the oil of cold-water animals and it became evident that, in particular, the oil in cold-water fish was of vital importance. Classified as Omega-3, this fish oil is apparently produced by small algae in the ocean and passes through the food chain, becoming concentrated in the tissues of cold-water fish like salmon and mackerel. The researchers noted that Greenland Eskimos who persisted with their traditional fish-based diet remained relatively immune to heart-disease. However, Eskimos who moved to eastern Canada and began to consume the orthodox high-fat western diet contracted the same rate of heart-disease as Canadians within a single generation!

Further data has also been compiled by doctors at the University of Leiden in Holland, who have been studying the link between heart disease and diet for the last 26 years. In a study of 872 men living in the small town of Zutphen, these doctors looked closely at the link between the consumption of saturated animal fats and the incidence of heart disease, and a recent survey of their data shows that the men who ate most fish lived the longest. For every ten deaths from heart disease among those who ate no fish, only four died who had been eating more than 40 grams of fish a day. What was interesting about the Dutch study was that subsequent research showed that lean white fish — relatively low in EPA — protected against heart disease as well as oily fish, so although EPA is an important ingredient, there could be other constituents, not yet isolated, which are also effective against cardiovascular complaints.

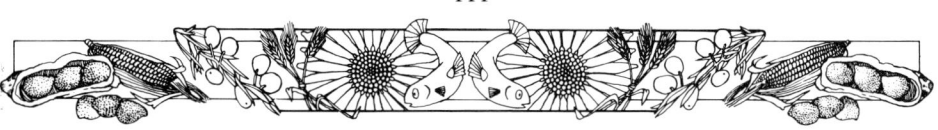

Why is EPA effective? The simple answer seems to be that because it contains a substance called prostacyclin, EPA helps to prevent platelets in the coronary arteries from sticking together. This helps to minimise the formation of blood clots which in turn lead to coronary thrombosis. EPA is a polyunsaturated fatty acid which gives rise to the formation of prostaglandins. These are important elements in the body chemistry since they are involved in such functions as gastric acid secretion, digestion, inflammation, allergic reactions and, in particular, blood clotting and thrombosis.

A recent study at St Vincent's Hospital, Sydney — the results of which were published in 1985 — showed that Omega-3 fatty acids help to reduce plasma cholesterol levels and also the levels of triglycerides in the body.* In particular, the more dangerous category of lipoprotein — low density, or LDL — is reduced, and the more favour-able form — high density, or HDL — increased. This study thus confirms the now widely held view that Omega-3 fish oils can help to protect against heart disease. Further studies have also shown that Omega-3 fatty acids are effective in treating rheumatoid arthritis and skin disorders like eczema and psoriasis. Omega-3 may also be effective in reducing the frequency of migraines and in aiding brain development.

The amazing thing about Omega-3 fish oil is that in a ten-day diet pattern, it appears to lower blood cholesterol levels by up to 20 per cent. So it may prove to be one of the major dietary medicines discovered this century!

*L.A. Simon, J.B. Hickie and S. Bala-subramaniam, 'On the effects of dietary Omega-3 fatty acids (Maxepa) on plasma lipids and lipoproteins in patients with hyperlipidemaia'. *Atherosclerosis* 54:1985, pp 75–88.

OLIVE OIL

The olive is traditionally regarded as a symbol of peace, for it was an olive branch that a dove brought to Noah, indicating that the Great Flood was receding. The ancient Greeks wore garlands of olive leaves in their hair as they prayed for peace, and olive branches form part of the booths erected at the Feast of Tabernacles in Jewish religious observance. Even in a modern political setting, it is an olive branch within a dove's beak which is depicted as a symbol of peace on the blue and white flag of the United Nations.

The olive tree, known botanically as *Olea europea*, is an evergreen native to the Mediterranean, and is thought to have grown on Crete and the Greek mainland over 5000 years ago. Olive trees thrive in warm and tropical climates and are now grown commercially for their oil in such countries as China, Greece, Italy, Algeria, Mexico, the United States, South Africa and Australia.

Olive trees rise to a height of around eight metres, have dark green and silver leaves, and fragrant white flowers. After fifteen years the tree bears fruit — oblong rounded drupes which turn from green to dark purple as they ripen.

The best oil comes from fruit which is nearly fully ripe, and hand-picked. The oil itself comes from the pulp, not from the kernel, and mills crush the fruit gently so that the stone is not fractured. In due course the oil is separated by centrifuging, and is filtered for purity. This is true 'virgin olive oil', but there are various grades of virgin oil, depending on the aroma and degree of acidity. The oil also varies in different regions of the world. Oil which is deemed to be perfect in flavour and aroma is known as 'extra virgin', while 'fine virgin' retains the perfect aroma but is more acid. 'Plain virgin' oil is even more acidic and its flavour is less pleasing.

In addition to these, further grades of oil can be produced with subsequent pressings, involving higher temperatures, hot water processes or solvent-extraction techniques. Such oil is still labled 'pure' but is sometimes blended with 'virgin' oil to improve its flavour.

Some Mediterranean and American oils are lighter in colour — pale yellow or light green — and have low acidity, while the oil from rich acidic soils is darker in colour. On the whole, pure oil is more stable

than virgin oil, and lasts longer, so blends are perhaps the ideal practical choice.

Olive oil is rich in unsaturated fatty acids, containing 73 per cent mono-unsaturated and 12 per cent polyunsaturated acid. Especially rich in oleic acid (which forms 72 per cent of its total fatty acid content) olive oil also contains 11 per cent linoleic acid and 0.7 per cent alpha-linolenic acid.

Olive oil is somewhat 'fatty' and 'heavy' among oils, and this enables it to be utilised in soaps and cosmetics. Olive oil also has several healing functions, both with internal and external use.

Olive oil is nutritious and easy to digest. It is often used in salads and is also ideal for cooking: it is consi-dered a healthy food oil because it increases the secretion of bile. Olive oil also acts as a laxative through its contracting effect on the muscles of the bowel. In addition, it may be applied externally to burns, sprains, bruises and insect bites, and can also be mixed with oil of rosemary to pro-duce an excellent natural treatment for dandruff. Combined with alcohol, it is useful as a hair tonic, and it also forms a base for several medicinal ointments.

For obvious reasons, olive oil is highly regarded in many different countries of the world. Olive trees grow to a venerable age, and serve as a perennial reminder that many of Nature's finest medicines are ever-accessible — if we just take the trouble to utilise them.

PUMPKIN SEED OIL

The pumpkin is a warm-weather vegetable with an ancient history: it is known to have grown in Central and South America up to 9000 years ago! Pumpkins were introduced to Britain from Turkey in the 17th century and feature in the famous children's tale *Cinderella*, in which a pumpkin serves as a fairy coach. Gypsies are said to eat pumpkin seeds every day to preserve male potency, and in North America, where pumpkins have grown since at least 1000 BCE, hollowed-out pumpkins are now associated with candle-lamps for Halloween.

Pumpkins grow best in fertile soil, especially near compost heaps, and do well on raised mounds of earth which provide adequate aeration and drainage. The flesh of the pumpkin contains Vitamin A, but it is the seeds which cluster in the centre of the pumpkin which are of most interest to us here.

Pumpkin seeds contain approximately 30 per cent protein and are especially rich in zinc, which is useful for maintaining the health of the prostate gland. The seeds can be roasted, salted and eaten as is, or crushed to make a dark, sweet oil. This is suitable as a food supplement in winter, since it fortifies the lungs and helps to resist bacteria in the mucous membranes. Pumpkin seed oil is also useful as a diuretic for urinary complaints, as a demulcent, and as an anthelmintic to expel worms from the intestine.

SAFFLOWER SEED OIL

The safflower (*Carthamus tinctorius*) belongs to the sunflower family. Also known as American Saffron, it is a tall annual with spiny leaves and orange, thistle-like flowers. Safflower is actually native to the Mediterranean region but the plant has been cultivated as far afield as ancient Egypt, China, India, and more recently in the southwestern regions of the United States. Safflower grows best in hot, arid or semi-arid climates.

Safflower has diuretic properties and hot safflower tea produces perspiration; for this reason it is often used to treat colds and similar complaints.

Safflower oil is extracted from the seeds of the plant and has a bland, slightly nutty flavour. Among natural food oils it is one of the least expensive and also has the highest percentage of unsaturated fats of all vegetable oils — around 76 per cent polyunsaturated and 14 per cent mono-unsaturated. It is especially high in linoleic acid (75 per cent) and also contains 0.5 per cent alpha-linolenic acid. This means that like other vegetable oils high in polyunsaturates, safflower oil helps to clear the arteries of fats rather than clog them with fatty deposits. Like most vegetable oils it is also rich in Vitamin E.

Unfortunately safflower oil becomes rancid if not stored in a refrigerator and is not suitable for deep-frying because its flavour is unstable at this temperature. It can be used in salad dressings and a drop or two added to the water when cooking rice or pasta will help to prevent it from sticking. Safflower oil produces a particularly high quality vegetable margarine and its valuable nutritional properties are being increasingly recognised.

SUNFLOWER SEED OIL

The sunflower (*Helianthus annuus*) is a native of tropical North and South America. It was prized by the Indians who ground the seeds of the flower with a pestle and mortar to make meal. They also used the oil extracted from the seeds both to grease their hair and to rub into parts of the body affected by rheumatism. Among the sun-worshippers of Peru, the plant was considered especially sacred and featured in religious ceremonies.

Sunflowers grow to a height of four metres and the seeds are located in the centre of the bloom, surrounded by bright yellow petals. Sunflower seeds may be obtained either mechanically hulled or unhulled, and ideally should be firm but not too dry or hard. They can be toasted and used with bread or vegetables as a snack. The seeds have also been used to produce a drink somewhat similar to coffee.

Sunflower seeds contain Vitamins A, D, B-complex and E and are also rich in such minerals as calcium, zinc, potassium, iron and phosphorus. Most varieties of sunflowers are suitable for producing oil, but the composition may vary according to different growing conditions.

Not surprisingly, the oil from the seeds of the sunflower resembles that of the safflower, to which it is related. Sunflower oil is approximately 53 per cent polyunsaturated and 33 per cent mono-unsaturated, containing between 50 and 70 per cent linoleic acid and 0.3 alpha-linolenic acid. (The exact proportions of linoleic acid vary depending where the flowers grow. The content is higher in cold countries like USSR, and lower in American or African varieties.)

Sunflower oil is considered to be an effective diuretic and is also good for building strong healthy teeth in children. It is a good cooking oil and can be used for frying, and in salad dressings.

The market for sunflower oil seems to be expanding. It is popular in Europe, America, South Africa and Australia, and vast acres of sunflowers are now cultivated for oil in the USSR.

SESAME OIL

Sesame, also known as *benne*, is one of the oldest herbs grown specifically for its seeds. The Chinese cultivated sesame some five thousand years ago, the Egyptians ground it to produce flour, and Roman soldiers mixed sesame seeds with honey to give themselves extra strength for their long and arduous military campaigns. In several Middle Eastern and Mediterranean countries, such as Egypt, Lebanon and Greece, sesame features in the cuisine in the form of *tahini*, a savoury paste, while *halva* is a Jewish confection made of sesame and honey. Sesame is grown and cultivated in many other countries as well. These include Africa, India, China, Thailand, the United States, and various Central and South American countries like Mexico, Guatemala and Brazil.

The sesame plant, *Sesamum indicum*, is an erect annual with white trumpet-like flowers. There are several different varieties which vary in height from 0.5–2.5 metres. The plant grows well in sandy, well-drained soil in a hot climate. In some instances harvesting begins while the seed capsules are still green, but when ripe the unhulled seeds are brown in colour. The hul-

led seeds, on the other hand, are waxy, creamy or pearly white, measure approximately 3mm in length, and are like a flattened pear in shape.

There is a certain amount of controversy over the presence of calcium oxalate in the hull of brown sesame, and some scientists have expressed concern that eating calcium oxalate may result in mineral depletion, kidney stones and even arthritis. For this reason the white, hulled form of sesame is preferred, even though this process causes a marked reduction in iron, potassium, and Vitamins A, B_2 and B_3.

Sesame oil can be extracted from normal seeds, or seeds which have been roasted prior to being pressed. The latter oil is dark and smoky red and is often used in Chinese cookery. The natural oil is light in colour, slightly nutty to taste, and ideal for dips, salad dressings, sautéing and deep frying.

Sesame oil contains 41 per cent mono-unsaturated fatty acids, and 44 per cent polyunsaturated, but contains only 42 per cent linoleic acid. However, this combination means that sesame oil is comparatively stable and does not become rancid on contact with the air.

Sesame oil enriches the blood and stimulates blood platelet count. In fact, twenty or so drops of sesame oil taken daily, doubles the blood platelet count in children in three to four weeks and is effective against spleen disorders. The oil is also high in Vitamin E, the B vitamins and the minerals calcium, magnesium and phosphorus. It is a good source of vegetable protein and is comparatively rich in lecithin and the amino acid methionine.

Because it is high in calcium, sesame oil is not acid-forming and is therefore an ideal laxative for those who suffer from stomach disorders.

SOYBEAN OIL

The Chinese have cultivated soybeans for over four thousand years and the beans are now used to produce a variety of traditional oriental foods. However the real breakthrough came when the Chinese, and later the Japanese, discovered that it was easier to digest soy protein if the beans were fermented. Shoyu, or soy sauce, for example, is produced by steaming soybeans and roasting and 'cracking' an equal quantity of wheat. The two ingredients are then mixed and inoculated with *koji* mould. Later the mixture is added to sea-salt and spring water, and the liquid is then aged for three years. The conversion of starches to sugars, and their subsequent interaction with natural yeasts to produce alcohols and esters, gives rise to the distinctive aroma of soy sauce.

Soybeans have a certain appeal because they are free of cholesterol, rich in lecithin, have a low ratio of kilojoules to protein, and contain almost none of the indigestible saturated fats found in most animal foods. Soybeans also have a comparatively low oil content (18–20 per cent) which lends itself to commercial solvent extraction.

Historically, soybean oil used to be imported mostly from China and Indonesia but the United States is now the largest exporter. The oil extracted from soybeans is dark yellow and comparatively high in unsaturated fatty acids (25 per cent mono-unsaturated and 60 per cent polyunsaturated). Of its fatty acid composition, 52 per cent is linoleic acid and 7.4 per cent alpha-linolenic. Soybean oil is a good source of Vitamin E, although it is not as rich in this vitamin as wheatgerm oil or sunflower oil. It has a strong flavour, which admittedly doesn't appeal to everyone, and is generally only used in baking and in salad dressings when a distinctive taste is sought. Prone to oxidation, soybean oil is nevertheless suitable for frying provided that the food which is cooked in it is eaten promptly, rather than stored for an extended period.

Despite its idiosyncrasies, the soybean is such an excellent source of protein and unsaturated fats that it is considered a natural vegetarian alternative to meat, and the high proportion of linoleic acid in soybean oil is an excellent antidote for cholesterol in the diet. The lecithin in the oil also helps to protect the arteries from fatty deposits.

Soybeans haven't always been as well received as they are today. In 1854, Henry Thoreau noted in his book *Walden* that the beans had been brought from China and cultivated in the deep south of the United States. There the farmers used soy to breed excellent livestock. If only they could have realised the health benefits soybeans also have for humans!

WHEATGERM OIL

Wheat is the most widely cultivated cereal grain in the world and is thought to derive from hybrid wild wheat which grew in the Middle East ten thousand years ago.

Most varieties of cultivated wheat belong to two basic types: *Triticum durum* and *Triticum aestiva* (or *vulgare*). The latter is used to produce bread, while *Triticum durum* is a harder type of wheat used to make semolina, spaghetti, macaroni and other forms of pasta.

Wheat grain consists of three parts: the bran, or outer husk, representing 12 per cent of the grain by weight; the germ (around 3 per cent) and the starchy endosperm (85 per cent). Milling for white flour separates the wheatgerm altogether and it is this wheatgerm which is especially nutritious, containing 25 per cent protein and an impressive array of vitamins and minerals.

Fortunately wheatgerm oil is now available as a natural food supplement. Rich in phosphorus, zinc, iron, potassium, sulphur and Vitamins B_1, B_2, B_3, B_6 and E — wheatgerm oil providing the finest source of Vitamin E — it is especially useful for neutralising acid and toxic wastes in the body. It also converts albumen to fibrin, which improves nerve function. In growing children it helps to maintain healthy spines, bones and muscles, and can be taken also to prevent eczema, indigestion and development of varicose veins.

Also, and most importantly, its anti-coagulant, anti-oxidant properties help to remove cholesterol deposits from the arteries and are thus of vital importance in combating heart disease. It is significant that wheatgerm oil has approximately 47 per cent of its polyunsaturated fatty acids in the form of linoleic acid, and 6 per cent linolenic acid, making it one of several useful food oils in the battle against low density lipoprotein.

SELECTED
BIBLIOGRAPHY

Addison, J. (1985) *The Illustrated Plant Lore*, London: Sidgwick & Jackson

Bach, E. & Wheeler, F.J. (1977) *The Bach Flower Remedies*, New Canaan, Connecticut: Keats

Bartram, T. (1984) *Nature's Plan for Your Health*, Poole, Dorset: Blandford Press

Bland, J. ed. (1983) *Medical Applications of Clinical Nutrition*, New Canaan, Connecticut: Keats

De Haas, C. (1986) *Natural Skin Care*, Sydney: Nature & Health Books

Drury, N. (1981) *The Healing Power*, London: Muller

Fulder, S. (1984) *The Handbook of Complementary Medicine*, London: Hodder & Stoughton

Grossinger, R. (1980) *Planet Medicine*, New York: Doubleday Anchor

Janssen, S. (1972) *A Guide to the Practical Use of Incense*, Sydney: Triad

Lesser, M. (1980) *Nutrition and Vitamin Therapy*, New York: Grove Press

Loewenfeld C. & Back, P. (1974) *The Complete Book of Herbs and Spices*, Newton Abbot, Devon: David & Charles

Love, R.V. (1986) *Folk Flower Tonics*, Kuraby, Queensland: Love Publications

Lust, J. (1974) *The Herb Book*, New York: Bantam

O'Mullane, J. & Muir, C. (1986) *The Fat Factor*, Wellingborough: Thorsons

Price, S. (1983) *Practical Aromatherapy*, Wellingborough: Thorsons

Reid, R.L. (1984) *Healthy Eating in Australia*, Melbourne: Hyland House

Rose, J. (1979) *Herbs and Things*, New York: Grosset & Dunlap

Ryman, D. (1984) *The Aromatherapy Handbook*, London: Century

Scheffer, M. (1986) *Bach Flower Therapy* Wellingborough: Thorsons

Tisserand, R. (1979) *The Art of Aromatherapy*, New York: Destiny Books

Valnet, J. (1982) *The Practice of Aromatherapy*, New York: Destiny Books

Vlamis, G. (1986) *Flowers to the Rescue*, Wellingborough: Thorsons

Walker, C. & Cannon, G. (1984) *The Food Scandal*, London: Century

Yudkin, J. (1985) *Encyclopedia of Nutrition*, New York: Viking